National Writers Series
Writers Series of Traverse City

2019 NATIONAL WRITERS SERIES LITERARY JOURNAL

Featuring work by the ...
2019 Scholarship Winners
Front Street Writers
Traverse Heights & Blair Elementary Fifth Graders
Creative Writing Middle School Students

The 2019 National Writers Literary Journal is a showcase of poems, stories and literary nonfiction pieces written by students in the Front Street Writers—an award-winning, rigorous and free writing program taught at the Career-Tech Center. A collaborative program with the National Writers Series, this workshop is a creative home for 28 talented and motivated high school students in the Grand Traverse region.

Also included are the winning pieces of the NWS college scholarship competition (a partnership of NWS and the Community Foundation); students enrolled in middle school creative writing classes (a partnership of Northwestern Michigan College and NWS); and NWS poetry writing workshops taught at Traverse Heights and Blair elementary schools.

Volume 5

National Writers Series

Copyright @2019

Published by

N W S
National Writers Series

National Writers Series
1200 W. Eleventh St., Suite 231
Traverse City, MI 49684

All rights reserved.

ISBN: 9781950659081

PRINTED IN THE UNITED STATES OF AMERICA

COVER DESIGN: Cover design by Carise New, graphic arts student at TBAISD Career-Tech Center

BOOK PRODUCTION: Mission Point Press
www.missionpointpress.com

For additional copies, please email your request to Cindy Weaver at nws.cweaver@gmail.com.

CONTENTS

Foreword   *vii*
About the National Writers Series   *xi*
About the Front Street Writers Program   *xii*
Acknowledgements   *xv*

2019 Scholarship Winners

Lake Ann in Three (or More) Fires
Seth Kirby   3

Gresham Soaring
Abby Riffell   10

To the White '95 Dakota Sport
My Sister's Father Used to Drive
Molly Stadler   17

Front Street Writers

It Will Be Okay
Shelby Brown   23

Done Deal
Sage Campbell   36

When I Get Home
Erin Evans   39

Shoe
Jaylah Ferris   44

Grandma
Jenna Ferris   46

Fur Real
Athena Gillespie   50

The Baby and the Ballerina
Hannah Gregory   62

The Thankless Mayor
Jonathan Gregory   75

Tango of Love
Mathew Hosler Jr.   89

Welcome
Rebekah Keeder   101

3,926 Mile Love
Camilla Kiessel   105

The House My Grandpa Built
Clara Kroll   109

The One Who Cries in the Bathroom at a Party
Clara Lick   115

Warm and Fuzzy
Joseph Lyons   119

Unwelcome Terrors
Joshua Makinson   124

Dragon Heart
Jesse L. Martin   129

The Place Where Good Men Go
Caleb Mitchel-Ward   132

Devil's Play
Zoe Moseler   142

America's Weakness
Zoe Moseler   144

An Epistle to Love
Reann Nelson   146

I, Too, Sing America
Reann Nelson						148

Six Hundred and One Seconds
Riley Kate Robinson					149

Head Over Heels
Emma Ryan						161

Horatius
S. E. Schneider						166

Last Breaths
Jacob Spann						170

Elle
Molly Stadler						177

Anxiety
Calista Trowbridge					180

Late Night Cigarettes
Adam Warner						182

The Girl in the Back Corner
Domnique Williams					195

Bad Dream
Dominque Williams					196

The Prince of Fire and Ice
David Yuhaus						197

NMC Creative Writing Workshops
Lost in Myself
Cici Copenhaver					207

Delphi – A Cursed Child Prequel
Gabrielle Parker					210

What's Around Us
Nora Riley   213
The Courage of Ophelia
Margaret Worden   218

Dead Bones
Eleanor Olds   222

Perspective
Talon O'Brien   224

Flowers for the Dead
Hannah Abner   227

Saroiny Jordan Hosler   230

Makenzie Womack   232

A Eulogy for the Common Sandwich
Eli Pszczolkowski   235

R.I.P. BLT ~ March 14, 2018 – March 14, 2018
Nathaniel Myers   236

Snape's Childhood
Kristen May   237

Fifth-Grade Poetry Workshops
Goodnight World
Aveelee Frantz   245

My Dog
Thomas Monroe   246

The Wet Blizzard   247
Nataliya Gorokhoviskiy

Foreword

By Front Street Writers Joseph Lyons and Shelby Brown

Joseph

There are moments in people's lives that stick with us forever. Front Street Writers has given me more of those moments to remember than anything else in my life. I came to this class as a senior. Unfortunately, that means I've only had this year to enjoy the class; I will always regret not applying my junior year. Still, the things I've learned and the friendships I've made here will stick with me for the rest of my life. I cannot put into words the total effect this class has had on me. When I started this year, I had a daydream of what I wanted to do after school: fiction writing. However, as we learned— it is a class focused on preparing us for a life as a writer— fiction may not pay well. After that realization, I came to the conclusion that I didn't just care about fiction; I cared about stories. Human stories pique my interest the most. Now, I'm going to be pursuing journalism for my career. I would never have discovered my love of interviewing, or the thrill of discovering a story, without this class. Front Street Writers saved me by giving me a purpose. I don't know what I'd be without the goals I've made for myself that were spawned from being a part of this amazing program.

The important thing to remember is that Front Street Writers isn't just for journalists, fiction writers, poets, or playwrights. It's for anyone who wants to learn more about the written word. That's another reason why I love this class. The diverse specialties that each student brings to the table is amazing. We have essayists, poets, detectives, journalists, prospective teachers. We also have people who want to pursue psychology or some that appreciate philosophy. The point is that what makes us great isn't that we are all the same, it's that we all have different interests and backgrounds that somehow complement each other in the most interesting ways possible.

Shelby

The thing that makes Front Street Writers such a special program for me as a second-year student is that there aren't many things like it. It's not only that we learn how to write, or that we meet dozens of successful writers; it's more about the community and creating confidence in the students. Every member of the program knew how to write before they joined the program, but we were convinced that we couldn't write well enough. We had the talent inside of us; we just needed some confidence and support and maybe a few more proofreaders to produce work that represents our full potential. I know that when I came into the program, I never thought of myself as a playwright or journalist or even a poet. It turns out I was all of those all along, but I had no clue. As writers, we need other people to help us open up and really blossom as artists. Before I joined the program, I was not comfortable with public speaking or performing. It was the one thing that was really setting me back from fulfilling my full potential as a student and a leader. Performance and discussion is a large part of the curriculum of the class, so I was required to step out of my comfort zone. Coffeehouses, workshops, competitions, and day-to-day discussions required me to gain some courage and confidence in public speaking.

Joseph

Front Street Writers is about student growth on an individual scale. Because of this there is a massive focus on the revision of our work. Our instructors read all of our work in detail and leave comments throughout the piece to try and point us towards areas of expansion. It's one of the reasons I respect the teachers so much. Most teachers just grade and go; there is no revision, just pass or fail. That's not how FSW works. Here we all help each other to be better than we were the day before. Workshop is a great example of this. During workshop we usually split into two groups where everyone is given a packet that includes the other students' work. Then we read a piece and leave notes usually centered on concrete imagery, and powerful writing. I was terrified about my first workshop. We were doing our poetry unit and I had no previous experience with poetry, which led me to the conclusion that I would be laughed out of the room as soon as it was my turn to be workshopped. Surprisingly that didn't happen. Turns out, everyone is nervous about sharing their work. My turn came and went without any laughter, and a surprising amount of compliments. (After the first workshop nerves started to fade), I even started to look forward to workshops because I was excited to see what my amazing classmates came up with.

Shelby

Remember thinking on one of my first days in the program that I would hate the class and the entire year because it was a new environment and I wasn't comfortable. I thought my classmates were more talented than I was. This year however, as a second-year student in the program, I put my leadership hat on for the first day to act as a friendly face to new students. As the year went on, I was able to watch as friendships were formed and confidence was built. Joseph and I built a relationship that was different than any relationship I've ever had with a classmate at my home school. My goal for every semester was to participate in discussion more, and although I grew in participating more as the years went on, I never really felt like I met my goal until this last semester while sitting by Joseph. It worked both ways. Joseph often raises his hand at every thought he comes up with, I acted as his filter keeping him focused on the current moment instead of daydreaming about clouds. He, for his part, encouraged me to volunteer in class more and pursue a train of thought that I wouldn't have pursued on my own. Ms. Collier theorizes that we work together this way because I am an oldest sibling and he is a youngest; that's one example of the types of relationships that the program encourages.

The program isn't really like a class, or at least like any class I've heard of or experienced before it. Ms. Scollon calls us her "darlings," and Ms. Collier has gotten into the habit of addressing us as "children," and every class period is started off with their asking us how we are doing. We answer with thumbs up or down. If someone is having a rough time, Ms. Scollon and Ms. Collier always have open ears. They listened to our cries of stress and our pleas for deadline mercy. I've had a lot of good teachers in the past, but none of the classes or teachers compare to this program.

Joseph

Shelby and I have grown quite close this year, sequestered at our table corner, and when I look around the room, our friendship is mirrored in the smiling faces I see. Relationships that normally never happen, because of the distance between our home schools, flourish in this class because of our like-minded pursuit and love of writing. I could not be more blessed for the amazing connections I've made while studying the arts here. I sincerely feel that I could call or text any one of my classmates after graduation and ask them for help in whatever my future plans may be.

About the National Writers Series

The National Writers Series is a year-round book festival held at the historic City Opera House in downtown Traverse City, Michigan. NWS is dedicated to bringing to life great stories and storytellers in an intimate and entertaining conversation. Our motto is: Turn a page, open the world!

At NWS, we believe that by leaning in around the campfire of a story, we engage the power of fact and imagination to reveal what it means and feels like to live in America today.

The National Writers Series uses net proceeds from its events to help support its Raising Writers programs, including Battle of the Books, a reading competition engaging 300 fourth- and fifth-graders; poetry workshops at Blair and Traverse Heights elementary schools; NMC writing workshops; and the NWS scholarship competition held in partnership with the Community Foundation.

About the Front Street Writers Program

Front Street Writers is a rigorous, for-credit and free-of-charge writing program held at the Career Tech Center. The program encompasses all aspects of the writing process, from early brainstorming and drafting, to a peer review workshop and thoughtful revision. Each student's goal is to create a portfolio of finished writing samples.

Throughout the year, nationally renowned authors who appear on the National Writers Series mainstage take time to visit the FSW classroom to talk about the craft of writing and their perspective of what is professionally possible. The mission of FSW is to lead students in making an imaginative life and a professional living as a writer. In 2017, this unique program received an Education Excellence Award from the Michigan nonprofit Set-Seg, which came with a $2,500 check to further strengthen the program.

Our 2018-19 students were taught in a workshop setting by acclaimed poet Teresa Scollon, a certified teacher with the Traverse Bay Area Intermediate School District, and award-winning playwright Sam Collier.

FSW students are required to go beyond writing in the classroom. They read at the National Writers Series events and vie for an NWS scholarship—a competition open to all students living in the five-county area. Their work can be found at www.frontstreetwriters.org.

The National Writers Series created Front Street Writers in the fall of 2012. Second-year students now have the opportunity to participate in professional writing internships in the areas of news reporting, editing, technical writing, copywriting, publishing, business writing, and corporate social media.

If you are interested in supporting the Front Street Writers or hiring a Front Street Writer intern, please contact NWS Executive Director Anne Stanton at 231-631-1551 or via email at nws.astanton@gmail.com.

For more information about the National Writers Series, please visit www.nationalwritersseries.org.

Acknowledgments

Front Street Writers is made possible by grants from the Michigan Council for Arts and Cultural Affairs and the National Endowment for the Arts.

We also want to give heartfelt thanks to the following donors who made the Front Street Writers program a reality:

Ross and Brenda Biederman and the Biederman Foundation
Audrey Adelle Bliss
David Bump
Casey Cowell
Bill and Susie Janis
Diana and Richard Milock
Smith Haughey, Rice & Rogge
Jon and Marissa Wege

The NWS Literary Journal is a team effort. Our thanks go to Samantha Collier, who served as managing editor. Thanks, too, go to Heather Shaw for the book production; TBA-ISD graphic arts student Carise New for the cover design; to C.D. Dahlquist for editing; and to Anne Stanton, who also edited and coordinated everyone's efforts. A special thanks to Sam Collier, who taught the poetry workshops held at Blair and Traverse Heights elementary schools, and to the wonderful classroom volunteers who helped out!

And, of course, thanks to all the young writers who worked so hard on their entries and had the courage to share with the public.

Thank you to all!

~ The Writers Series of Traverse City Board of Directors

2019 SCHOLARSHIP WINNERS

2018 Winner of the Community Foundation
Leslie Lee Nonfiction Scholarship Award

LAKE ANN IN THREE (OR MORE) FIRES
By Seth Kirby

When my brother Sean and I had first moved into our family's new apartment in Lake Ann, Michigan, it was hot. So unbearably hot. We'd just come back from a Boy Scout summer camp, complete with horrible plumbing, humid outdoor tents, and enough bug bites on every square inch of our skin to draw constellations. Needless to say, we were at the peak of discomfort.

Our parents and two younger siblings were already stationed at the house long before that day. They'd been setting up the entire house for at least a month in advance. The apartment was relatively small, so moving everything from our spacious property back in Swartz Creek into this second-story building would prove a daunting task—one I would be glad not to participate in. Still, it didn't feel right not setting up our rooms. At some point, I thought that maybe the new house would be a pleasant surprise, or at least something to fill in the gap of the old one. Something that when the curtains were pulled, I could say "Oh gosh, I never would have thought!" That was the hope, at least.

>>>>

Of course, hope flickers easily.

>>>>

The first settlers of Lake Ann (also known as Almira Township) were named John and Alec Heather, who came down in 1862. However, no one built a single building until later that year, when settlers Andrew and Almiral Burrell built a house near the northern edge of Sancrainte Creek, a place somewhat northwest of Lake Ann known generally by the name "Sancrainte Hill." They would be the first of many to build the foundations of what would be Almira Township.

>>>>

Dad had moved to northern Michigan around September of 2014, a year before our arrival. He took some bare necessities, a few keepsakes, and a good portion of packed-up luggage. He started working at the job he'd managed to get: a head chef position at a Baptist summer camp. The rest of us stayed back in Swartz Creek, continuing the packing process while my dad made the new house livable.

I remember becoming a second father to my family, stepping in to help when Mom had trouble filling the role of two parents. After school, I would clean the house the best I could. I would read a story to my brothers and tuck them in, if I remembered. And I knew it wasn't Dad's fault. This was just how transitions worked. We would sometimes Skype with Dad, crowding on our parents' bed around the one laptop in the house, watching him laugh as we reenacted any scene we could think of: Darth Vader killing Obi-Wan (Obi then hiding under a blanket as his robe hits the mattress); a TV salesman attempting to sell spray-on Cheez Whiz; and pirates sword fighting with pillows. Part of it was we were trying to cope with the distance. The other part was just to fill the gap—the one that, for young boys, couldn't be filled by anything except a father. Maybe it worked?

Still, it was a long year.

>>>>

The first, most disastrous fire in Lake Ann History broke out on the 4th of July, 1897. The fire destroyed more than 88 buildings, the town's main depot, almost 2,640 feet of railroad track, and a mass of homes, too many to count. Almira Township's firefighting force was not enough to combat the heat, and nearby Traverse City was telegraphed for reinforcements. The fire started in the engine room of Habbler Sawmill, belonging to one William Habbler. The mill was one of the most prominent sources of income for Lake Ann.

Many people died. Lake Ann's population before the fire was around 1,000. Afterward, in the low hundreds. Charcoal bodies dotted Almira, to be cleaned up in the aftermath (though they never found all of them). Almira was slow to recover from scars of the fire. Blackened supports were nailed together with wooden beams. Scorched walls were merely painted over. Shadows left behind by the buildings and people never quite faded.

>>>>

The day we found ourselves together again at our new house, standing around a white plastic table baked in heat, was the Fourth of July in 2015. We had settled in as best as we could, though every room was incredibly small. The apartment was a second-story addition to a historic building that had been around for several centuries and long since converted into a party store.

My parents had not intended to have us there during the Fourth of July, but some God-ordained force allowed it to happen, I guess. Traverse City, our neighboring city, was hosting a festival known as the National Cherry Festival. Held every year for a week in early July, the actual holiday was the obvious summit of events. There were many attractions: live bands, hot food, and carnival rides. The problem was, they all cost money. Having recently moved into a new house, cash was a little tight. So, the only real reason Mom brought up the idea of the festival was to watch the Fourth of July fireworks together.

Our family typically had a hard time getting all six members into the car in a timely fashion. Because we had nothing to do, however, we were perfectly fine with rushing all at once down the creaky set of white wooden stairs, shaking the shoddy steps so hard it seemed they would collapse. We piled into Dad's black SUV, which had baked outside under the glaring sun for hours on end. We didn't seem to mind.

>>>>

The second fire started during 1914, the same as the first. William Habbler had purchased a second mill father northeast from Almira, promptly after the last fire had taken place. This was presumably an attempt on Habbler's part to avoid starting another town-razing fire. Sadly, his plan didn't work. The fire, in part, grazed over some of Habbler's unfixed damage, merely finishing the job. The rest of the fire destroyed Lake Ann's business district, already partly decimated by the last fire. Once again, the repairs were flimsy and lacking. Even though the fire took significantly fewer lives, it was no less harsh; many of the damaged businesses later suffered from poor structural integrity, some threatening collapse.

>>>>

Before the fireworks, our busy bodies needed fuel to burn. So we decided to travel to a bar and grill, somewhere close to the outskirts of Traverse City. The place was surprisingly packed for an "outskirts" kind of place. One of my younger brothers, decided not to order his meal, instead resorting to drawing on his kid's menu with some crayons. Halfway during the meal, he was aggressively filling in some large drawing with a red crayon. He pushed too hard and the crayon snapped.

My brother was old enough that random accidents didn't make him cry. Still, he whined to Mom about his crayon crisis. She told him to just use the blue one instead. My brother, upset, wanted the waitress. Our parents were understandably against the idea: it was a busy night, and the waitress was on the other side of the restaurant. My brother fussed and pestered, but we eventually got him to calm down. By the time our waitress returned to the table forty-five minutes later, my brother had wrapped the two rosy crayon halves in paper napkin. He didn't care. When we eventually left the cool restaurant to walk toward the fireworks show, the heat hit us hard. It was as hot outside as that morning had been, and I hoped that my large dinner wouldn't be making a guest star appearance in the night's fireworks display.

>>>>

The third and last fire was in 1918 and probably the most forgiving. It only managed to cover less than half of Lake Ann, which excludes the previously burned business district. This fire burned down the prominent Congregational Church, leveled several nearby homes, and (for the third time) completely ruined William Habbler's Sawmill. The firefighters of Almira were able to put out the flames alone, but the damage to the church and the mill had already been done. They were never rebuilt to what they were.

>>>>

The fireworks were going to start in a few minutes, and we had completed our long walk through town. It had been an exhausting trip, but I had tipped a jazz musician playing beautifully on the street, so I felt content. As we came upon the beachfront, we passed another man: this time, on the ground with two officers. The man was hammered, one officer at his side while another in a neon green safety vest talking over a radio. Others around me had been drinking, some even drunk.

I started to speculate, something my brain decides to do at the worst possible moments. I wondered if the man might be an angry drunk, who would get up at any moment and knock the two officers flat. Maybe he would run into the crowd and start hitting people, hitting me. It may have been because the situation was so unfamiliar, but I started thinking up strange situations, things only feasible to a stressed and tired mind. I pictured the fireworks coming at us and singeing the beach, making people run all over. My mind was in a perpetual blur.

And in an instant, a bright red light shot up into the sky, followed by a sharp boom.

>>>>

It started like a chain reaction.

The third fire started in the residence of Alex Frazer. More specifically, it began in Alex's defective chimney. That night, he must have set a large fire. A strong wind heading northwest caught some of the embers and carried them to many of Almira's resident's houses, lighting aflame every roof it touched. Those fires created more embers, which were carried away to create more flames. Eventually, the embers set afire the Congregational Church. It was truly horrifying. It was fascinating. A brilliant part of Mother Nature's final raid on the town.

>>>>

Each and every explosion left me in awe, each color within a color, each yelling burst of chemicals. I was watching the night sky come alive. And most importantly, I stopped thinking—about people or weapons or hiding from killers. All my thoughts were about what I was straining my neck so hard to see. The fireworks did its job. And I'm glad it worked.

That night, something distinct happened in my brain I can only vaguely remember. Because the apartment was small, we had to double up two brothers in each bedroom. I was stuck in a poorly-inflated air mattress with Sean. The room was humid, the fan provided no cooling, we both sweated in the summer air. The scene looked and felt a lot like it did at the beginning of the day. I turned my eyes toward the nighttime stars outside. I thought back to the fireworks, and my mind began to wonder in the way that it does. I thought of how hot fireworks get when the explode. I thought about how they even make fireworks, and what happens to the cardboard after you set one off. And even though the room was so unbearably hot, my 13-year-old mind slowly drifted away....

Works Cited

Benzie Area Historical Society and Museum. History of Lake Ann Michigan. *Facebook,* 29 October 2018, www.facebook.com/BenzieAreaHistoricalSociety/posts/1853552298215130. Accessed 8 November 2018.

"History" *The Official Website of Almira Township,* www.almiratownship.org/history.asp. Accessed 8 November 2018.

Leary, Richard. "One Hundred Years Ago: Lake Ann Devastated by Fire, 1918." *Grand Traverse Journal,* 1 Apr 2018, www.gtjournal.tadl.org/2018/one-hundred-years-ago-lake-ann- devastated-by-fire-1918/. Accessed 10 November 2018.

Seth Kirby
Interlochen Arts Academy, 11th Grade

GRESHAM, SOARING
By Abby Riffell

Gresham liked books. He always had.

He liked the way his glasses slipped down the freckled bridge of his nose when he read, as if he was being sucked in, bit by bit. He liked learning about insects, or tsunamis, or magic wardrobes. He liked the way that words spun around his brain and filled up all the quiet spaces.

In fact, one could say that Gresham *loved* books.

Though he enjoyed reading about them, Gresham was rather friendless himself. Most of the other ten-year-olds in his class did not love books; they were too preoccupied with showing off their new phones and pelting dastardly aimed spitballs at the teacher's sweater. They were confused by Graham and how he opted to shove his nose in a book instead of joining them on the swings. He had no siblings either, unless he counted Herbert, who was seventeen years older and directed sloppy film adaptations of perfectly good novels. His parents were nice people, the kind that made their own pie crust and polished their briefcases, but they were not people with time. And besides, they were far fonder of Herbert's movies than they were of Dickens.

So, Gresham read.

He had learned many years before that his questions would not get a reply. Of course, if he would ask something simple, such as "Mother, are we out of milk?" or "What time is dinner?" there were always answers in supply. But Gresham already knew what time dinner was, and it was always quite obvious if one was out of milk or not, so the only questions he had left were the ones for which he did not have any immediate answers. At first his parents and teachers were amused, hailing him as clever, a genius even. This did not last long. They soon tired of discussing, say, metamorphosis, or post-war reconstruction, and would instead hand him a book. It was easier than telling a child no taller than the cosmetic bureau that they hadn't the slightest idea.

So, Gresham read.

He read about the free-market system, phytoplankton, and heroes. He read about love, time travel, and geometry, and every time he had a new question he would read some more. His father would crane his head over the back of the recliner, one of Herbert's films flashing from the television, and look to his wife with a chuckle.

"Reading another one of those books," he'd say, and turn back to the screen, confident that Gresham must be very content indeed. Gresham's mother would hum a nod, then return to the movie.

Gresham, however, was not completely content.

He wanted a friend.

Monday after Monday slid by, along with the school year, and Gresham was beginning to worry; he did not want to spend another lonely summer helping his mother make pie crusts. He thought about this as he walked to the library on a particularly rainy day—big, frustrated droplets smacking at his umbrella—until he reached the establishment. Gresham grabbed the brass doorknob, tarnished and worn by the hands of hungry minds, and pulled.

>>>>

It was seven o'clock at night and Gresham, though clad in his pajamas and comfortably nestled underneath his quilt, could not sleep. He could not sleep *at all*.

"I did it." he whispered to himself, "I really did it!"

He rolled to his left. From his bedside table, a biography of Teddy Roosevelt glared up at him. "I did it, Teddy." He whispered again, the picture of the president unmoving in reply. "I found a friend!"

Gresham's stomach plummeted at his own words. He still did not know anything, not even a teaspoon's worth, about being someone's friend. He hadn't had a real friend since first grade, when Max Turrel moved away to Idaho. What if she didn't want to be his friend anymore, once she figured out that he was completely deficient?

Yes, his new friend was a girl, and she was beautiful. He met her at the library, which he believed was fate, if not an act of God.

He first saw her, perusing the non-fiction section. Her skin was a color he had never seen before, except in books; it was dark, like hot chocolate, and her teeth were perfect rows of glistening pearls. The whites of her eyes popped against her skin, making it hard for Gresham to break eye contact, his gaze always floating back to their brightness. Gresham wished that more people in his world looked like her. He wished that he was not so pale and freckled, and instead had half-moon dimples on cocoa cheeks. He wished for his dark, flat hair to spring up in wild curls a and a gap to appear between his pearly front teeth.

"Why are you staring at me?" she said, interrupting is thoughts. Gresham froze. He had not anticipated that she would actually notice him.

"I- I didn't mean to, I-," he stuttered as she chewed at her lower lip and cocked her head.

"Never mind," she said, interrupting him. "I'm looking for a book about Georges Mèliès. Have you seen one around here?"

She chattered on, lifting to her tiptoes to read the titles on the top shelf. "He created some of the very first movies, like ever."

"I know." Gresham replied quietly, deftly sorting through the second row of books. "My brother talks about him all the time. He makes movies, too."

"Wow," she said, pulling free a burgundy colored book. She gave the title a quick scan and then slipped it back onto the shelf, letting out a "Tsk" of impatience. "I bet your brother talks about Mèliès to make himself sound smart. I've heard that directors are like that sometimes."

Gresham looked to the floor for a minute, blinking. People were usually impressed with his brother, but then again, most people couldn't pronounce Mèliès correctly either.

"Ah," the girl said, returning to the balls of her feet. "I think I was rude again. I'm sorry. I keep on telling my mouth to stay quiet, but lately it just ..."

"It's fine." Now Gresham had his turn to interrupt. And he was smiling. "You're right. And Herbert—that's my brother—turns all of my favorite books into love stories. Anyways."

He stiffly reached out his hand, which was clutching a biography of the famous filmmaker.

This was his moment to make an introduction.

"Here's your book." *Come on,* he urged himself. *Just your name.*

She thanked him and took the book, and then she was gone before he had time to say anything else.

Gresham groaned. He had been so close.

"Oh, I almost forgot!" A head of wild curls popped back around the corner. "I can't believe that I made a friend and didn't even think to introduce myself." She smiled and half-jumped, half-slid over to Gresham in her excitement. "I'm Layla."

Gresham didn't really remember much of what happened next.

All he knew was that he ran all the way home, arms spread wide—an eagle- heart spinning like a reel of film. Soaring.

>>>>

Honey was a woman with fire in her belly. That's how Layla described her grandmother to Gresham on their way to her house on a sunny, green, Tuesday afternoon. Even though they had been playing together for weeks, this was the first time that he had ever gone over to her house. With each footfall, Gresham tried to make sure each shoe hit each sidewalk square only once. Being of very small foot, and the squares quite large, it was turning out to be a more difficult task than he had anticipated, so he was too preoccupied to really think about what she said.

What? Fire can›t be in bellies, he thought distractedly before brushing it aside. He was coming to realize that when Layla talked, she said things that weren't actually real. But they were always true, so Gresham assumed that he would find out what she meant when he actually met Honey. He wasn't expecting flames, but he repeated *stop, drop, roll* in his head a few times over, just in case.

Earlier that morning he and Layla had tumbled into his house, with bare knees stained from slides in the grass, breathless from their race inside. At the sight of their soiled glory, his mother exhaled an abrupt cough, the same noise she made when her dough didn't rise properly in the oven.

"Gresham," she warned in exasperation. "I've already told you to stop running around in all that dirt. You've gone and stained another shirt."

Gresham, though breathless moments ago, found himself suddenly too full of air, as though all of the panting and sprinting were being sucked back inside of him.

"My Grandma says that running around is good for kids," Layla piped up. Her cheeks still held the luster of their romp, and her eyebrows perked up confidently. Gresham could tell that she had something more to say, and his stomach flipped. As far as he could tell, she didn't have any qualms about challenging grown-ups.

"That's nice," his mother replied evenly, filling two glasses of orange juice for them. Gresham, however, could sense her surprise. He knew that she was not used to children who disagreed.

"Yes," Layla continued matter-of-factly, taking a sip of juice before setting down her glass. "Honey—that's her name, you know—says that if you don't let us run around when we're kids, we're just going to run away as adults."

Layla, seemingly undisturbed, took another sip. "What do you think?" she asked Gresham's mother, who had paused with the refrigerator door half-open, the juice carton still in hand.

"I think...," his mother trailed off, returning the carton to the refrigerator.

Gresham eyed both his mother and Layla nervously. He didn't want his only friend and his only mother to argue.

"I think that it sounds like Honey would appreciate your conversation. Why don't you two head over and talk to her?" his mother said, shooing them. Her wrists were spindly and her palm flung about in the air dramatically as Gresham and Layla rose from their seats and made their way to the front door, orange juice abandoned. "Run along now."

Gresham halted. He could not help but remember the philosophy book he had read the previous week. *That's called tu quoque,* he thought, *when someone says one thing, only to act in an opposite manner.* He opened his mouth in response, for he could not help but address the lapse in logic. "But you just said that I shouldn't be running."

"Gresham, you know what I—oh! There go my pies—burning!"

His mother gave the two children a dismissive wave, hurrying them outside. Clearly, she was not in the mood to philosophize.

So that is how Gresham, on a Tuesday afternoon, found himself counting sidewalk squares and wondering about the nature of Layla's flaming grandmother. He looked up from his feet, wincing as one of them stepped on a crack, at the shouts of Layla. She had picked up the pace to a run and was headed toward a compact bungalow situated on the far corner of the street. On its front porch stood a tall woman with broad shoulders, which were shaded by a wide-brimmed gardening hat.

Quickly, Gresham surveyed the house and the woman on the deck, who he could see now was smiling. There were no traces of smoke, and he did not hear the crackling of flames. *So far, so good.*

Abby Riffell
Elk Rapids High School, 12th Grade

2019 Winner of the Robert and Marcy Branski Poetry Award

TO THE WHITE '95 DAKOTA SPORT MY SISTER'S FATHER USED TO DRIVE

By Molly Stadler

When you were there
Parked haphazardly, not quite between the lines
On the blacktop of the Meijer parking lot
It meant he was there
Sitting in your driver's seat, staring at us through
Your windshield

I can still see you
And the colorful faces
On the slab of wood my grandfather painted
Zip-Tied to your grill
And caught between headlights

I remember you
Outside my second home
Beside the neighbor— his friend's house
Whose music blared when it got dark; and in front of
The tiki torches he insisted to buy which
Eventually caught fire sometime
Late at night

You meant trouble in my six year old mind

You were idle
On the pavement
Waiting outside his work while
We came to visit him
And you stood still as voices grew
Icy, harsh, loud
And palms slammed against windows before
He jumped on the hood of my
Mom's car as
We tried to drive away

You lounged in the shade
Underneath the mulberry tree
At the third house
Watching through the little window on the door
As he shoved my mother down the stairs
My sisters and I crying as she stood up, and
Rushed us to the bathroom
Locking the door behind her before
He started beating on it

You froze
Like a scratched DVD
While he became some sort of animal
Climbing up the terrace of the 4th home
And trying to break in
While my sisters huddled together
Locked in my room, listening
To my mother's screaming

And you never
Hit the gas to crash—
To run him over, no
You just watched.
Like a child on Saturday morning

Molly Stadler
Front Street Writers/Career Tech Center
Home School: Grand Traverse Academy, 12th Grade

FRONT STREET WRITERS

IT WILL BE OKAY
by Shelby Brown

CAST OF CHARACTERS

MANDY   Twenty-eight years old. Wife of ERIC and mother of TOMMY. Has red hair and fair skin.

ERIC   Twenty-six years old. Husband of MANDY and father of TOMMY. Has dark hair with a crew cut.

TOMMY   Four years old. Son of MANDY and ERIC. Has messy, dark brown hair.

Scene
A family home at two in the morning during the summer.
A small storm is passing through.

Time
The present.

Scene 1

AT RISE: ERIC and MANDY are asleep in their bedroom late at night. The curtains are open to the small storm brewing outside the window.

ERIC stretches his arms and then turns his body toward MANDY and wraps his arm around her lovingly. As he does this, lightning illuminates the room and a loud boom of thunder is heard.

MANDY (violently pushing ERIC)
No! NO! Don't touch me! Don't touch me! Stop!

(ERIC lets go and moves back away slightly.)

ERIC
I'm not doing anything wrong! It's me, your husband! It's okay.

MANDY (panicked)
You're not my husband? I don't have a husband!

ERIC
Mandy. Shhhh, it's me, Eric. We're married and have a son together.

MANDY (calmly)
Oh, I guess I forgot, I'm sorry.

(MANDY leans into ERIC.)

ERIC
It's okay, baby. Lie back down, it will be okay.

(MANDY looks around the room.)

MANDY
Mister, where am I? I'm scared.

ERIC
Eric, my name is Eric. There's no need to be scared.

MANDY
I'm s-scared, but I don't know what of and I—and I don't like it.
>(MANDY looks at ERIC in panic. MANDY moves quickly away from ERIC.)

Oh, dear God. Oh no. No! No! NO!

ERIC
Shh. It's okay! It's okay, honey. It was probably just a bad dream. Just a bad dream. Shh. It's going to be okay.
>(ERIC lets go, stands up and takes a step back.)
>(MANDY is shaking on the bed and curled up in a ball.)

Did you take your meds?
>(MANDY ignores ERIC's question.)

MANDY (muttering)
He won't leave me alone. Why won't he leave? Why won't he? He won't go. He won't go.

ERIC
Who won't go?
>(ERIC reaches down to touch her.)

Who is he?

MANDY
No! No! No! No! Back!
>(ERIC pulls his hand away and takes a step back.)

ERIC
Okay... Okay... I'm back here. Tell me what he did.

MANDY
No. He won't like that. He won't like that. No.

ERIC
Okay, just tell me who *he* is then. Please, I won't tell. Please.

MANDY
He's... He's... He's...

    (Lightning illuminates the room.)

    (Thunder is heard.)

    (MANDY looks up at ERIC and points.)

He's you!

    (MANDY stands up and confronts ERIC while ERIC backs away with his hands in front of him.)

MANDY	ERIC
You! You! You're him!	No! It's me! It's just
Get away! Get away!me!	Your husband!

    (MANDY takes a step closer to ERIC and looks him in the eyes.)

MANDY
Please help me...

    (MANDY buries her head into ERIC's chest.)

    ERIC (rubbing her back)

It's okay. It's okay.

MANDY
I'm so sorry. I-I'm just tired. I must have been dreaming.

ERIC
Okay, yeah. Let's just go back to sleep.

    (ERIC leads MANDY back to the bed.)

MANDY

O-okay...

> (MANDY's eyes begin to close as ERIC lays her on the bed.)
>
> (Lightning illuminates the room.)
>
> (Thunder is heard.)

No! No!

> (MANDY begins to fight and scream at ERIC.)

Don't touch me! Help! Please help!

MANDY	ERIC
Stop! Stop! Help please!	Shh. Honey, it's me, Eric. Your husband, it's just me. Shh.

> (MANDY stops fighting ERIC.)

MANDY

Oh. Oh no. I'm sorry

> (MANDY leans into ERIC and weeps.)

I'm s-s-s-sorry.

ERIC

It's okay. It's okay. Shh... Shh... Look at me.

> (MANDY looks up at ERIC.)

It's going to be okay. Now, what's going on? What happened?

MANDY

I-I-I don't know. I'm just scared, b-b-but I don't kn-kn-know what I'm scared of. I want it to stop, Eric.

ERIC

It was probably just a dream. It was just a dream. Just a dream.

MANDY
Okay... Okay, yeah. Just a dream.

ERIC
Let's go back to bed, okay? If you have another dream, just wake me and we can talk about it? How does that sound?

MANDY
Okay.

(ERIC helps MANDY onto the bed. ERIC covers MANDY with a blanket and tucks her in.)

ERIC
Try to get some sleep.

(He leans down and kisses MANDY on the forehead.)

MANDY
Okay.

(ERIC sits on the edge of the bed until she is asleep.)

(Once MANDY is asleep, ERIC rubs his eyes and talks quietly to himself.)

ERIC
What is going on? My wife has gone nuts, and who even is this guy?

(MANDY mumbles something in her sleep.)

What was that, Hun?

MANDY (slurring)
W-w-we ca-can just kill him.

ERIC
Uh. Mandy, we're not killing anyone. Who do you want to kill?

(MANDY answers in incoherent mumbles.)

Mandy, Sweetie, you're worrying me...

MANDY
No. No, it-it's okay.
ERIC
No. No, you can't kill anyone.

MANDY
Tommy will ... will be fine with me.

ERIC
What about Tommy? Mandy, what are you talking about? Honey, answer me!

MANDY
I didn't have a dad, I'm just fine.

> (ERIC stands up and paces the floor with his hands on his head and talks to himself.)

ERIC
My-my wife ... is talking about ... killing me. My wife wants to kill me. What am I supposed to do? I need to call someone. Just in case. Out of love. I'm doing this out of love ... and fear, mostly fear.

> (ERIC picks up the landline phone from the nightstand and dials a number.)

PHONE
911, what's your emergency?

ERIC (quietly)
Hi. Uh, I don't know how to say this, uh, but my wife is acting, really strange. I'm kind of worried.

PHONE
Strange? How, sir?

ERIC
I don't know. She's talking in her sleep and she's talking about this man and freaking out on me.

PHONE
Are you in any immediate danger, Sir?

ERIC
I-I don't know!

PHONE
Well, sir. Did you do anything to upset her? Did she have a few drinks? These are all pretty common things. If you don't give me a better reason for your call, I'm going to have to ask that you settle your marital problems on your own.

ERIC
No! No!

>(ERIC is facing away from MANDY. MANDY opens her eyes and sits up but remains quiet.)

She's talking about killing someone! And... and she is acting like... like... like a psychopath! I don't know what to do and I'm- I'm freaking out!

PHONE
Okay, Sir. Just calm down, we'll send someone out shortly to check up if you're that worried abou—

>(ERIC turns around to see MANDY taking her hand off the receiver base of the landline phone.)

MANDY
What are you doing?

>(ERIC removes the phone from his ear.)

ERIC
I-I was... making sure we were safe. I was telling them about him. So, he can't hurt you.

MANDY

Are you sure?

ERIC

Yes, of course. Would I ever lie to you?

MANDY

I don't know. Come back to bed.

ERIC

Yeah, of course.

>   (ERIC puts the phone back on the receiver base and gets into bed.)

MANDY

Goodnight.

ERIC

Goodnight.

>   (ERIC closes his eyes.)
>
>   (Lightning illuminates the room.)
>
>   (Thunder is heard.)
>
>   (MANDY stands up and reaches under her pillow and pulls a knife from behind the pillow. MANDY walks around the bed and stands above ERIC.)

MANDY (chant-like)

Just kill him. Kill.

>   (ERIC opens his eyes.)

ERIC

Honey, what are you doing?

>   (Lightning illuminates the room.)
>
>   (Thunder is heard.)

                              MANDY
Kill. Kill.

    (ERIC sits up and moves away from MANDY.)

                              ERIC
You're scaring me, Sweetheart.

    (MANDY moves closer.)

Help! Please! You're scaring me!

    (MANDY moves closer.)

HELP! PLEASE HELP! HELP!

    (Lightning illuminates the room.)

    (Thunder is heard.)

    (MANDY attacks ERIC. ERIC screams.)

                              MANDY
No! No! NO!

    (ERIC screams as MANDY continues to stab him until she kills him. MANDY looks at ERIC and then at the knife in her hand. There's blood down the front of her nightgown.)

Oh, no. What have I done?

    (MANDY moves away from ERIC's body.)

WHAT HAVE I DONE!

    (There's a knock on the door.)

                        TOMMY (offstage)
Mommy?

    (MANDY hides the knife behind her pillow and opens the door. TOMMY stands in his pajamas with tears streaming down his face. MANDY shuts the bedroom door behind her and hugs TOMMY.)

MANDY

It's okay, baby. You're okay. It's okay. Mommy is okay. Let's get you back to bed.

> (MANDY leads TOMMY back to his bedroom offstage.
> MANDY re-enters the stage.)

What am I going to do with him? Oh my.

> (MANDY picks up the sheets from the bed and uses them to clean up the blood.)

I'll wrap him in the sheet and bury him, there we go. That's what we'll do.

(END SCENE)

Scene 2

> AT RISE: MANDY is at the side of the house with a shovel and ERIC wrapped in a sheet. It's dark with the exception of distant street light.
>
> MANDY begins to dig.
>
> MANDY digs for a few minutes before she begins to speak.

MANDY

It's okay, no one is going to know. He left me. Husbands leave their wives all of the time, right?

> (MANDY stops digging and looks toward the garage.)

The car... they'll know he didn't leave without the car! I'll just crash it somewhere. I'll sell it! There we go, there we are.

> (MANDY continues to dig until the hole is big enough to fit ERIC's body. MANDY pushes the body into the hole.)

Okay. Okay! Everything is going to be okay.

(MANDY puts the shovel and knife into the hole with ERIC.)

No one will know.

(It begins to rain hard.)

Oh, dear God.

(MANDY begins to use her hands to cover up the body and evidence.)

(Sirens are heard in the distance.)

(END SCENE)

(END PLAY)

Shelby Brown, Senior
Kingsley High School

DONE DEAL
by Sage Campbell

It's the day I have been fretting about all year. If I've made the right choice, it won't end well for me. If I've made the wrong choice, it won't end well at all.

I shove my thoughts away as I walk down the road. I have to get to the coffee shop before Eli can. He will definitely kill Andrew without hesitation. Why did I tell them to meet up with me at the same coffee shop? Not to mention that I told them to meet me at the same time. That wasn't part of my assignment! My mission was simple, but no. I had to go and mess everything up.

A white van with some logo for electricals honks at me as it pulls out of an alley. *Crap. They found me.* I get out of their way, only to turn down the next alley. I tuck behind a dumpster as I hear the van turn into the alley. The doors open and slam shut four times, but I only hear six feet hit the pavement. *Someone is trying to be smart with me.*

I peer my head past the dumpster to see if my assumption's correct. Ten men surround the van. John and Vincent are there, of course. John is in his usual stained tank top. He always wears that when he's on the hunt, which means that I'm on his hit list. *Shoot. How did you get yourself into this pit, Akari Naoko?* But it isn't John I'm worried about. It's Vincent.

John has always been the classic Big Bad Boss, with Vincent as his little rat. Where John is muscular, Vincent is crafty. Where John chooses pure strength, Vincent prefers tools, knives, and guns, and only gets dirty when he thinks he's won. John will preoccupy the victim and tire him out, and Vincent will come in when least expected. I'd have to be a foolhardy idiot to not be scared lifeless at the sight of them on my trail. I grew up watching them drag their "catch of the day" back to the sewers that we called home. I grew up watching them torture poor souls who had fallen too far in the wrong to be reconciled.

I grab the stun gun from my belt before deciding on my homemade tear gas. *Good thing I decided to wear layers.* The other eight men are in all black with an array of pistols and knives strapped to them. I lean back out of sight before one of them can get even so much as a glimpse of me.

"Come on out, Akari. We know you're here." John's voice is thick and booming. "Get out here before you do something you'll regret." *Too late.* At that, Vincent smirks. I can feel it. I take a deep breath and pull out the pin in my tear gas bomb, tossing the bomb so it bounces off a wall to distract them. I watch as it rolls right up to their feet. *Just like in the movies.* "What th—!" An explosion of tear gas cuts him off. Immediately a chorus of coughs and commands begin.

I grab the collar of my jacket and hose it down with my water bottle before covering my nose and mouth with it. I know the gas will still sting, but it'll help. I grab my grappling hook and wrap it around the back handle of the dumpster and take off. I run around the coughing group of men, looping the rope around anything big, heavy, and slightly portable. After reaching the dumpster, I tie a slip knot with the rope I had tied earlier. *Now for the hard part.* I get into a crouch and rush to the back of the van. My eyes and lungs burn, but I have to get it done. The guys will find me in any moment, and I have to finish this trap. I tie the rope on the bumper of the van before bolting out of the cloud.

Just as I am about to get out, a hand grabs my wrist. I jab my heeled boot into his foot, twisting around to increase the pain, only to see pain and sadness in Vincent's face. *Sorry, old friend, but I have to go.* His hand releases me, and I whip off my jacket, tying it around his arms before he can react. Then, I'm gone, but not before I hear all of the men running into their van. The doors close, the van starts, and as they slam on the gas everything that I had tied that rope to slams into the van. Those screams were really what I needed today.

I sprint to the coffee house just as Eli begins to make his way toward Andrew. I catch a glimpse of Eli's dagger and get an idea. I grab the coffee pot from an unsuspecting waitress as I rush behind Eli, pouring the hot contents on him. Eli's pained screams draw Andrew's attention to us. Eli whips around to me and his fist nearly makes contact with my stomach. *Too predictable.* I bring my knee up as I force him down. My knee meets his gut half way, releasing a grunt from Eli. Andrew makes eye contact with me, shrouded in confusion.

"Annie?"

"Get out of here, A—." I'm cut off as Eli charges me, throwing me toward the wall. The wind is knocked out of me as I hit a table. Plates crash and shatter to the ground. People are running out of the shop, but Andrew is staying in place, his eyes locked on me. Eli straightens, chuckling.

"Annie? Is that your name now, Akari?" Eli's voice is filled with pleasure, and threat. Andrew's eyes dash between me and Eli.

"Andrew, get out of here," I groan.

Eli turns back to me, smiling madly, his knife glinting in the light. As he goes to make a slash through me, I lean back and kick him in the chest, hearing the air leave him. He falls to the ground and I go to run past him, to Andrew. Eli wraps his hand around my ankle before I can get away, and I let my heel meet his face for the first time. A satisfying crack leaves his nose as his scream fills the shop.

I turn back to Andrew and see horror written all over his face.

"Akari? As in Akari Naoko? As in the infamous villain Akari 'niece of the man who killed my mother' Naoko?" Betrayal enters his voice, and all I want is to take his pain away, but I have to finish my mission.

"You really need to work on your background checks," I say, smirking.

"Why — How — Why would you do this? How did you do this?" Fear. He's almost where he has to be. He staggers down the stairs, toward me.

"Your father killed all of my family. I've come to return the favor." I'm not sure if this will kill him first, or me.

"No. You're good. I know you—."

"That's where you're wrong. You know nothing about me. I'm evil. You're good."

"But the carnival ... that night on the rooftop ..." He stops, merely inches from me and Eli.

"All ploys to get your trust." Originally, they were, but they turned into the first moments when I felt truly happy. When I felt loved for the first time since my family had been murdered in front of me.

Hurt crosses Andrew's face. "I won't let you win this fight, then."

He grabs Eli's knife and stabs it into me. Shock and horror cross his face, but a smile only spreads across mine. I grab the knife to feel the weapon that is the cause of my downfall.

"Good choice. The same one used to kill my baby sister." I laugh, painfully, before entering the final stage of life. I don't see a light, but a shadowy figure. I grin even more. *I finished my mission. I made the right choice.*

Sage Campbell, 11th Grade
Glen Lake High School

WHEN I GET HOME
by Erin Evans

You shouldn't have gone out on the water when it was so rough, Tracey.

My mother's voice keeps playing through my head—everything she's going to say to me after I get back.

I've told you that a hundred times, but you never listen, do you?

I pull the tiller as hard as I can, making the boat swerve and tilt, a wave knocking into the side and breaking over the edge, where it sloshes on the deck, pooling around my feet. I squint up at the black sea in front of me, and can just barely make out the wave, bigger than I noticed before—at least twice the height of my sail. I didn't see it coming in the dark, and now it's close. I can already feel the water heaving under my boat as it is tugged back.

"I know what I'm doing, Mom," I say. "Don't worry, I'll be fine. I wouldn't have come out here if I didn't know what I was doing."

I move the tiller again so that I'm pointing directly into the wave.

You should never go out on the water when there's even a chance it might storm.

"This isn't a storm, Mom. There's no rain."

There's only wind. It wasn't here ten minutes ago, and now it's all I can hear as it wails around me and snatches my breath from my chest. My hands are freezing, fingers clutched around the tiller.

I shove them into my coat pockets as I take one more look at the approaching wave. It now stands only a few hundred feet away, black water gleaming as it towers above me.

"Okay, okay, let's think through this, Tracey. Turn the boat into the wave. I did that already. Okay, okay—oh, someone said to go below deck but I don't know if that's right and—I don't *have* a below deck, so it doesn't matter. Start thinking clearly Tracey. Think. *Think*.

The bow of the boat suddenly lifts, and I scream, dropping to my knees and grabbing the mast. I bend my head to my chest and shut my eyes.

The boat is thrown to the side as ice water crashes onto my back and breaks over me. I am wrenched from where I sit and lurch forward before more water hits me and I am slammed onto my stomach on the slippery wood of the deck. I gasp and try to grab on to anything with my nearly numb hands but there is nothing. I open my eyes but still can't see anything and more water keeps coming down and the boat tips, and I slide across the deck, clawing at the wood to no avail. My back hits the rail and I twist my body and grab it with one hand, before the boat is tossed onto its other side, lifting me off the deck so I am hanging in midair. My grip won't hold, and I struggle to reach the rail with my other hand, but I can't. My hand comes lose and my nails shriek against the metal of the railing. I flail in the air for a moment before the side of the boat comes back down, smacking the water and catching me as I fall. I hear something snap and feel a shocking pain in both of my legs, and I lie there, chest heaving, coughing up water until I can't breathe. My whole body shudders and I lie still for a moment, feeling nothing but the pain in my legs and the freezing wind rushing over me, stinging my body and pulling my sopping, tangled hair.

You could have been killed! You can never go back out on that boat again, or I swear to Jesus, Tracey, I will disown you. No daughter of mine gets to be that stupid—

That's what she'll say when I get home. I push myself up on my elbows and look all around the boat. No more waves as far as I can see.

"All right," I say. My voice is hoarse, and I cough and clear my throat. "See, Mom? I survived that wave. I told you I know what I'm—"

That's when my eye catches on something unfamiliar. The top of the mast is lying on the deck a few feet from me. It landed near a splintering hole in the boat, out of which water is pouring onto the deck. As I watch, the boat creaks and sinks an inch or so deeper into the water.

"No, *no!*" I yell.

What did I tell you about getting such an old boat? It's not safe, Tracey. I knew you should never have taken it out, I knew it.

"No, no, no—" I turn to see that the mast landed on my legs when it fell, and struggle to move out from underneath it. I limp as fast as I can to the hole and try to cover it with my hands, but it's much too big, at least a foot in diameter. I glance at the water. I could jump overboard and swim, but it's too cold and the shore is too far away and it's so dark and I'm so lost that I would have no idea which way to go. I grab the piece of the sail that ripped off with the top of the mast and try to cover the hole with that, but it's like trying to use a tissue to stop a bullet wound from bleeding. I feel my throat tightening and I would be crying if I weren't so panicked.

I told you you'd die out there, Tracey. One way or another—

"I'm not going to die out here." I try to laugh, but it's hollow and unconvincing. I lie back on my stomach, my head on the deck, and stare at the water filling my boat, spreading across the already flooded planks. There's something sitting, submerged, a few feet from the hole.

The radio.

I laugh for real this time, crawl over to it, and pick it up. The antenna is bent but should still work. I twist the dial as quickly as I can to turn it on and listen.

All I can hear is the wind and the waves.

"Come on, come on." I twist the dial again and straighten the antenna. It doesn't look broken. So *why won't it work?*

I told you that just because you have that little radio doesn't mean you're going to be safe.

"I know, Mom, I know. But I know how to use this thing. I'll get help and I'll be fine. I know what I'm doing here."

My hand starts to shake and the radio drops back into the water, which is now nearly up to my shoulders while I'm sitting down. I use my arm to bring the radio back and hold it between my knees. I press my hand into a fist against my thigh, unable to move it by itself, and smack it against the radio, as if hitting it will somehow make it work. I listen. Any sound at all would be good news. *Anything.* But it remains silent.

The boat creaks again, and I start spinning the dial in circles with my wrist as the water reaches my neck. I reach down and clamp the radio between my wrists instead of my knees, so it is above the water and use my chattering teeth to turn the dial again and again and again.

I'll never let you go back out there again, Tracey.

I can just imagine her telling me that when I get home.

"Okay," I say. "I'll never sail again if I don't have to." I keep turning the dial.

I don't want you to die out there, so I'll never let you go out again.

That's what she said last time, and that's what she'll say this time. That's what she always says.

I can no longer feel the floor of the boat underneath me. Only water. I kick my feet and tilt my head back, keeping the radio clenched in my teeth by the dial, and move my hands through the water, though I can't feel them. I can't feel anything anymore except my face, and even that is starting to go numb. My head is shaking so badly that the radio drops. I try to move to get it back, but it sinks too fast and I can't see anything. A wave slaps against my face, and I sputter and cough. I look out at the ocean around me. Everything is black. I look up. Through my shaky, blurred vision, I see the stars, and smile. I always loved watching the stars over the ocean.

I told you not to go tonight. I told you it was a bad idea.
That's what she's going to tell me.
"I know, Mom. I know."
When I get home this time, I'll listen to her.
I try to move my legs, but I can't feel anything.
I told you, Tracey. I told you to stay off the water.
When I get home, that's what she's going to say.

Erin Evans, 11th Grade
Bellaire High School

SHOE
by Jaylah Ferris

You put me on your feet like a worthless piece of property.
I know it's in my job description for you to place your feet in me,
    but I deserve to be treated with respect.
I have feelings.
You bought me because you loved me, and that's what made me
    love you.
It was love at first sight.
Now... I don't know what to feel.
Is our connection fake or real?
We have our good and bad times, but what may seem fun for you
    is not fun for me at all.
Jumping in puddles.
Fun for you.
Bad for me.
Not only being suffocated by the stench of your feet, but also
    suffocated by water.
I am drowning in filth.
I get to explore new places, but places that may be beautiful to
    you are not beautiful to me.
I get the gross view.

You can see the world!!
I can feel the world...
Rocks embedded in the wedges of my soul.
Painfully stuck.
As time goes on, you appreciate having me around.
You show me off.
Others copy your style
And now I have more friends.
I am not alone!
I have had my time.
Days become weeks ...
Weeks become months ...
Months become years ...
A new brand is in town, and he is making an impact on my life.
He is the enemy.
The brand-new style.
Bright white
Shiny logo.
As for me, I am dirty, old, and worn.
You liked him better —now you're wearing him.
You have forgotten about me.
Now I am alone again.
Nowhere to go.
You have moved on.
I lie in the dark closet.
Now it is time to rest.

Jaylah Ferris, 11th Grade
Traverse City Central High School

GRANDMA
by Jenna Ferris

The beach is and always will be my grandma's happy place. Sitting at the beach, peacefully letting the sun touch every inch of her body, reminding her that the world isn't always cold and cruel, she listens to the waves crashing down, leaving a hard slap on the rough yet comforting sand. With a subtle smirk tattooed to her lips and her eyes closed, she remains in her chair. The wind whispering in her ear seeks attention, and the shining sun brightly illuminates every object in sight.

The sun, which started out calm and warm, over time begins to harshly burn, causing a few sweat-drips to caress my grandma's slightly chiseled face. Eventually she can't take the heat much longer; she gets out of her chair and treads the hot sand that wraps around her feet like socks until she plants her feet in the cool welcoming waves. Each step she takes gradually makes her lighter, to the point where she slides onto her back, floating with her head peeking above the water. After letting the water hold her for a while, she stands up and walks back to the shore where she now carries her own weight. The sun, once overly confident as the day went by, is now shy, and will hide itself behind the Earth till dawn cracks the next day. Grandma packs her multi-colored striped chair, her vibrant red and white cooler, and her pink towel in her wagon made of wood and red metal, leaving her happy place to come to the less peaceful, less soothing, not as warm place we call home. The place which, in the summer, is my happy place: there's air-conditioning, food, and a power outlet.

Her beach day has now come to an end, and she walks through the gate that blocks off our property. The loud click of the gate closing is heard from inside the house and the next thing heard is the thumping of feet similar to a herd of elephants hitting the ground. *Thump thump thump* ... the sound of we teenagers doing our last-minute chores that we "forgot" to do during day and then racing back to our original positions on the couch or the floor. We're hoping to maintain a normal breathing pace when Grandma walks in the door and asks: "Is everything done?" and we simply reply: "Yes." As soon as the feeling of being proud of what we've done in such short time has had its pleasure, Grandma starts going down the list: "Clothes taken care of? Pajamas picked out? Towels and washcloths in the bathroom?" We confidently nod our heads up and down. The list isn't really done, and she asks: "Did you pick out your clothes for tomorrow?" and a hush falls over the room. After cooling down from running all around the house, there's a heat flash, and it's not because of the weather—it's because we're scared. "What does this mean!? No phones!? No T.V!? No hanging out with friends!? What!!!?" She tightens her eyebrows and folds her arms in disappointment and says: "Why are you still sitting here? GO!" And with that, there are two fewer people in the room. After a long relaxing day at the beach she comes home, does the laundry and cooks dinner, just in time for the moon to claim the night. We all close our eyes, eagerly waiting to see the next day of our happy place.

Wrapped around half her waist lies a scar. A scar that represents the hard times when she was able to push through the pain. Yes, the reason we have scars is from witnessing pain. In my mind the idea of a scar is that it once caused pain, but when it's touched, we find that there isn't as much pain as when we first got it. The sight of it may cause pain, but the pain has only made us stronger. My grandma got this scar from a lung cancer procedure in which the surgeons removed a third of one of her lungs that contained cancer cells. The scar is a little lighter than the rest of her skin tone. It has a silver outline like the outer rim of the sun, the moon, and the stars. The scar feels like driving over a speed bump in the road.

This scar is a reminder that she was fortunate to have a second chance at living a healthier and longer life. She had the option to decline the surgery, but either way she could've died. During the surgery, she could have ended up dying during the procedure, in addition to the surgeons not being able to get all the cancer cells. Another option would've been to not have the surgery, but she would have had to fight against cancer's deadly weapons. However, my grandma already has the armor needed to fight cancer — she's a strong and powerful woman. Grandma always says, "I may be small, but I am mighty," and there is nothing that will ever make me doubt it.

Four months of constantly feeling sick, taking pain pills, and sleeping all day, every day, she wasn't allowed to go to the beach or sit in the sun for long periods of time. When someone undergoes such a process of surgery and treatment, their skin is very sensitive to the extreme heat that the sun gives off. They were a long four months for her. She's the type of person who, if she wants something done, has to do it herself, no matter how much she wishes other people would do more to help. She couldn't have too many visitors at once because her white blood cells that fight infection were very weak and she could not risk getting sicker than she already was. Not only did she have to avoid people with germs, but the rest of the family did, too. My sister and I couldn't spend the night at a friend's house, go to the movies, or go to the mall. My grandma has never watched so much T.V. in her life. She could watch movies and shows that might have beach scenes, but she couldn't live her own movie as the main character sitting at the beach. After five months were over she was notified that she was cancer-free. She cried enough tears of joy to create her own lake. Receiving such great news was one of the happiest moments in our family. The next day, I went to school and told all my friends. I was so excited that I probably told them more than once. My grandma can go to the beach and sit in the sun for as long as she wants.

Every now and then I'll give my grandma a hard time, but I do truly love her with every part of my heart, and I trust her with my life. I am forever grateful for her and wouldn't trade anything in the world for her. She is mine, she's my rock, my go-to, my shoulder to cry on, my inspiration, my happiness, my sadness, and my love—and she always, *always* will be my grandma.

Jenna Ferris, 11th Grade
Traverse City Central High School

FUR REAL
by Athena Gillespie

CAST OF CHARACTERS

REBECCA	Sixteen years old, basic white girl, desire for things to go her way
MRS. DALE	Forty-two years old, mother of
REBECCA	loves dogs
BAXTER	20 years old (2.8 dog years), clumsy, loves eating everything, charming obliviousness
WOMAN	
MAN	
CHILD	
ANGRY PEOPLE	One or two actors acting angry in the background. Can be played by the same actors as WOMAN and MAN.

Scene
A stereotypical subdivision, a house with a white picket fence, spacious yet cozy inside.
A dirty, ugly, trash-filled street.

Time
Present day

Scene 1

> AT RISE: A spacious bedroom with pink walls and chewed up shoes scattered around the floor. REBECCA is waking up.

> (REBECCA yawns and stretches arms out, smiling)

REBECCA
Finally, I'm sixteen! This is gonna be the best day ever!

> (REBECCA gets out of bed and steps right into dog poop)

REBECCA
AHHHHHHHHH!! BAXTER YOU STUPID DOG!

> (REBECCA hops to bathroom and throws her socks away)

REBECCA
Wow, what a great start to my birthday. God I hate that dog. Breathe, Rebecca, you're good. Today is going to be amazing.

> (MRS. DALE muffled voice from offstage)

MRS. DALE
Honey, the chocolate chip waffles are ready! Your favorite!

REBECCA
Coming!

> (REBECCA walks downstairs into kitchen to find dog eating spilled waffles off the floor)

REBECCA
Are. You. KIDDING ME? BAXTER IT'S MY FREAKING BIRTHDAY! CAN I HAVE ANYTHING WITHOUT YOU RUINING IT?

(MRS. DALE walks into the room)

MRS. DALE

Oh dear... here let's clean this up and you can come open your presents! I can make more waffles later, I promise, sweetie.

REBECCA

Thanks, Mom, but Baxter gave me his gift early: he took a dump in my room. I really should clean it.

MRS. DALE

Oh heavens, that silly puppy. I'll go clean it, Becca, you open your presents!

(MRS. DALE exits room, REBECCA picks up a giant present off the table)

REBECCA

Whoa, this is heavy. Almost as heavy as you, you obese rat.

(REBECCA glares at dog, then opens present)

REBECCA

OMG OMG OMG! YAYYYYY! I've been wanting this for so long. And there's no way you can chew this up, HA.

(REBECCA pulls hover-board out of box and sets it on the floor. MRS. DALE enters)

MRS. DALE

Be careful honey! You don't want to run over Baxter's paw. Aw, look at the sweet baby.

(BAXTER drools all over couch. REBECCA rolls her eyes)

REBECCA

Yeah, what a sweetie.

(REBECCA gets on hover-board, wobbling and trying to keep her balance)

Whoa, this is kinda hard. WOOOOOOOOO! I'M REALLY GETTING THE HANG OF IT!

>(REBECCA zooms around quickly)

>>MRS. DALE

Rebecca! Please don't hurt yourself!

>>REBECCA

THIS IS AMAZING OH MY GOSH THANK YOU MOM I LOVE YOU SO-

>(BAXTER runs in front of REBECCA, causing her to fall and hit her head on the counter)

>>MRS. DALE

Rebecca? Rebecca? Are you all right?? You don't look so good...

>(REBECCA lies on her back, eyes slowly shutting)

>>REBECCA

That stupid dog ... I wish dogs never existed.

Scene 2

>AT RISE: A dirty street filled with angry people.
>
>REBECCA is sitting in the middle of the street. She opens her eyes and looks around.

>>REBECCA

Where the hell am I?

>(A WOMAN steps on her foot while walking by)

Hey! Ever heard of being polite?

>(A young blonde MAN appears beside REBECCA. She stares at him curiously)

53

BAXTER
No, she hasn't heard of being polite. No one has.

REBECCA
Um, do I know you? And what are you talking about? Also, where am I? Do you—

BAXTER
Oh, you don't recognize me? I'm your dog. In human form.
(REBECCA closes her eyes)

REBECCA
Okay it's official. This isn't real. This is a dream. Soon I'll wake up and be out of this hideous place.
(A fight breaks out in the street. The yelling startles REBECCA)

BAXTER
This is as real as those pink Uggs you have. Well, had. I chewed them up.

REBECCA
Wait a minute. How do you know about my shoes? Are you like a stalker or something? Back off. I have ... pepper spray!

BAXTER
Nice try, but I know you don't. I buried that in the yard, remember?

REBECCA
So ... you really are ... Baxter?!

BAXTER
Yessss ma'am! At your service!
(A CHILD kicks REBECCA, and spits on her. People are stomping all around her)

REBECCA

What the—okay "Baxter," am I in hell or something? I knew I shouldn't have stolen my aunt's Starbucks gift card. Karma's a b—.

BAXTER

You're actually in a world where dogs don't exist. So yeah, pretty much hell.

REBECCA

What? Why is everything so nasty and awful? And why are people so mean here? Shouldn't everyone be happy since there's no dog poop to clean up? And now that no one is eating their homework?

BAXTER

Not exactly... let me show you just how different your life is now. Follow me.

REBECCA

Oh boy, my own dog taking *me* on a walk? What a treat.

>(REBECCA rolls her eyes)

>(BAXTER whips his head toward her with all his attention focused on her)

BAXTER

Did someone say treat?

>(BAXTER leads REBECCA down the street, pointing to a small movie theater with holes in the walls.)

REBECCA

Wait, what movie are they showing? Does that marquee say... *SHARKNADO #87: SANTA JAWS*? Who would make such a monstrosity?

BAXTER

Well, you see, without dogs, producers had to find other animals to make movies about. So, *Marley and Me, Lady and the Tramp, 101 Dalmatians:* none of those cinematic masterpieces were ever thought of. Heck, you can't even have the *Wizard of Oz* without Toto!

REBECCA
I didn't realize how vital dogs were to the film industry. Good thing it doesn't affect me!

BAXTER
Screens weren't the only things injured by lack of pups. Let me show you to our next stop.
> (BAXTER walks down the street, leading REBECCA to a group of people throwing rocks at each other)

REBECCA
What's going on? Why are they so violent toward each other? I don't understand.

BAXTER
Unfortunately, dogs were never here to show people how to love generously. Kindness and happiness are unheard of. There are no golden retrievers to pet, no pug faces to squish. No fluffy friends to cuddle with. There's simply no joy in this world.

REBECCA
So, no one is nice to each other? Not even neighbors or friends?

BAXTER
Nope. There is a lack of bonding between neighbors because cookouts don't exist. There are no hot dogs to grill. And friendship? No one here knows what it means to be a friend; they have never encountered the perfect example of a loyal companion: man's best friend. Dogs.

REBECCA
Whoa, bro, slow your roll. Dogs didn't impact life *that* much, did they?

BAXTER
Just look around. Would you want to live in a place like this?
(BAXTER turns away and starts walking)

REBECCA
Wait for me! Where are we going now?
(REBECCA follows BAXTER across the street to a small, rundown shack. They dodge flying paintball pellets)

REBECCA
What's this?

BAXTER
This is your mother's home. Mrs. Dale! Where you at?
(MRS. DALE crawls slowly out of the shack, looking at REBECCA with confusion)

REBECCA
Mom! Thank goodness you're here. We've got to escape this nightmare ASAP!

MRS. DALE
Huh. You do look a lot like my daughter. Her name was Rebecca. Oh, how I miss her.

REBECCA
Mom! It *is* me! It's Rebecca!
(MRS. DALE pauses, and then shakes her head)

MRS. DALE
No, my daughter died at the young age of four years old. She drowned. Please, just leave. I don't want to be reminded of it.

REBECCA	MRS. DALE
Mom, wait! Please, just listen!	I SAID GET OUT OF HERE!

(MRS. DALE slams door closed. REBECCA looks at BAXTER with confusion)

BAXTER

Don't you remember? Your mother took you to the beach as a child, and while she was sunbathing, you ran straight into the water. But you didn't know how to swim, so you were struggling to breathe. Right before your body was going to give out, your old dog Buttercup ran and lifted you up out of the water with her mouth. She saved your life.

REBECCA

So just because troublesome little fur balls don't exist, my mother is living in a box, her own daughter is dead, and she HAS A PERM??

BAXTER

I wasn't there to eat the 80s hairstyle magazine. This was your wish, and it came true. But you still don't seem happy. Isn't this everything you've ever wanted?

(REBECCA glares at BAXTER)

REBECCA

No, this is horrible! Baxter, how can I get out of here? I miss my mom, my house, my phone...even you. Well, the dog version. You *were* pretty cute sometimes, even if you destroyed everything I owned.

(BAXTER sighs)

BAXTER

If only there were a simple solution.

(BAXTER pulls a collar with a keypad on it out of his pocket.)

I found this on the ground, but you're going to have to figure out the password. My small brain is definitely incapable of brainstorming, so you're on your own.

REBECCA

This will take forever! It could literally be anything. Hmmmm, what? I just type in a bunch of random letters!

>(REBECCA grabs it and types frantically. The red light on it beeps loudly)

BAXTER

Ohhh yeah, one more thing. The fine print on the inside of it says, "ONLY THREE WRONG ATTEMPTS BEFORE EXPLOSION!"

REBECCA

DUDE! Would have loved to know that BEFOREHAND! Anything else that might completely determine my fate?

BAXTER

Oh yeah. It also says, "HINT: WHAT IS YOUR DOG?"

REBECCA

How is that a hint? What is my dog? A freaking brat. A nuisance. An uncontrollable animal.

>(REBECCA types in the word "annoying." The collar beeps and the red light flashes)

BAXTER

I don't think that's what it wanted to hear. Also, I'm not *that* annoying! Remember all those times I ate your veggies off your plate when your mom wasn't looking? And every day after school I would wait at the window for you? And how my tricks always cheered you up? I really was a—

REBECCA

Good boy. A GOOD BOY! BAXTER YOU'RE A GENIUS! Good boy!

>(REBECCA types in GOOD BOY and the light flashes green. Everything starts to darken. Braxton waves good bye.)

Bye Baxter! Thank you for everything! I'll see you late—

>(Everything blacks out)

Scene 3

> AT RISE: A stray hover-board spins slowly next to REBECCA, who is lying on the ground in her kitchen.
>
> MRS. DALE stands over REBECCA. BAXTER licks her face)

REBECCA
Oof, my head is pounding.

MRS. DALE
Rebecca! Thank God you're okay! You passed out for a couple minutes after hitting your head! I was about to call an ambulance!

REBECCA
Mom! You remember me! Whew, scariest dream of my life. Baxter? Come here, boy.

MRS. DALE
Oh honey, I know you're angry at him. I hate to say this, but if you really want, we can give him to Grandma. I don't want him threatening your safety or anything, I'm so sorry this hap—

> (REBECCA hugs BAXTER and kisses his head)

REBECCA
Actually, I'm not angry at him. He's too cute to stay mad at anyway! I was thinking... can we get another puppy? It's my birthday after all...

> (MRS. DALE laughs)

MRS. DALE
Rebecca! Of course, we can get another! Haha, I'm so glad you've had a change of heart about Baxter. He really does love you, you know.

REBECCA
I love him too. You know, dogs make the world spin round.

(BAXTER looks at audience and winks)

THE END

**Athena Gillespie, 11th Grade
St. Francis High School**

THE BABY AND THE BALLERINA
by Hannah Gregory

CAST OF CHARACTERS

ELLA   Twenty-five years old. Is a former ballerina who misses the stage and is devoted to CLARA.

CLARA   Three months old. Is the daughter of ELLA and ANDY.

SHERRY   Sixty years old. Is the mother of ELLA and is enthusiastic about ELLA's career.

ANDY   Twenty-eight years old. Is the husband of ELLA and the father of CLARA. Works for a tech startup and is absorbed by it.

Scene
An apartment in Chicago, Illinois; a house in Michigan.

Time
The present.

Scene 1

> AT RISE: A dark bedroom in an apartment in Chicago. Thunder crashes and CLARA is crying. ELLA hurries into the room and goes to CLARA.

ELLA
Shh, shh, shh. Don't cry. Shh. Mama's here. Don't cry. Please don't cry. Mama feels so awful when you're sad.

> (CLARA stops crying.)

That's better, little one. I guess you woke up, huh. You woke up and cried for Mama, didn't you? Well, Mama's got you.

> (ELLA picks up CLARA.)

Oh! You are getting so big, pumpkin. Look at you! Mama has to hold you with two arms now.

CLARA
Mmmmmm-ma. Mmmmmm.

ELLA
Mmmm-ma? What are you saying? Maybe you're saying Mama, smart girl. And that's right. That's so right. I am Mama. And who are you? You are Clara, of course. And it's a beautiful name.

CLARA
Mmmmmm-mmmmm.

ELLA
Do you know who you're named after, baby girl? You are named after Mama's very first leading role: Clara of the Nutcracker. Oh pumpkin, I wish you could have seen me. It was perfect. My costume was gorgeous, the music was beautiful, and I felt so wonderful, spinning and leaping in the center of that stage. I was so very young then, only thirteen, and all the older girls were terribly jealous when I was picked. Absolutely everyone I knew came to watch me dance, and they all told me what an amazing Clara I made. They were all so supportive of me back then. My parents

swore that by the time I was eighteen, I'd be the prima ballerina of some prestigious company. And I believed them. I believed every single, wonderful thing that they said about me.

> (ELLA doesn't appear to notice as CLARA begins to whine. ELLA hugs CLARA closer.)
>
> (Wistfully)

I so badly wanted to be the brightest star in ballet. But I don't think that all those well-meaning adults were telling the truth, baby girl. I wasn't extraordinary. Oh, I did the movements well enough, and God knows I had the passion but... I just didn't have that spark. You know, that little glimmer of genius that somehow transforms a dancer from a human being into a bird or a fairy or pure fire. It's that little bit of magic that creates truly amazing stars, and I just don't have any.

> (ELLA shakes her head and sighs. CLARA's whines grow louder.)

But it doesn't matter, I suppose. I've done well, haven't I? I mean, I did join a ballet company and I've been in several productions. Never the lead, but someone's got to play a supporting role, right? We can't all be princesses; some of us must be the peasants. And I did enjoy it. I truly loved every second I spent on every stage, even though the audience wasn't really there to watch me. It was all so completely amazing. It's just... I always thought that someday, the director would see me. That he'd look and not see this twenty-something try-hard, but instead a beautiful and earnest artist whose imperfections maybe even added to the effect. I thought that one day, it'd be my chance to be in the spotlight. If I just stuck around long enough, I'd get my chance.

> (CLARA begins to cry. ELLA rubs CLARA's back and CLARA quiets.)

Do you know what, baby girl? Last night, I found some old pictures of me. They were hidden in a shoebox that was tucked in the very back of the closet. I didn't even know it was there. There were so many photos in that box: twenty years' worth. One was from when I was five, dressed in a fluffy pink tutu for my first dance class, another was from my first day dancing professionally at eighteen, so serious in a plain black leotard. And at the very bottom of the stack, I found a picture taken about a year ago, when I was a swan in Swan Lake. That was my last role, you know. About a month later, I found out that I was having you and... I had to stop performing. Anyway, in that photo of my last dance, I'm crouching in a tiny dressing room with stage make-up slathered all over my face. My arms are draped around a few other dancers dressed in silvery leotards, and I am beaming. I'm grinning toothily at the camera, and I look so, so happy. Last night, staring at that picture, I realized something. I can't go back to being that elated ballerina. My entire career... Well, it's pretty much over. It's done, and I'll never be seen now, because I had you, little darling. And you mean so, so much to me. I'd never trade you for anything, not even for all the Sugar Plum Fairies in the world. But it still hurts to think that I won't ever return to the stage. It's impossible to even pretend that I'd be allowed to. My company won't want me, not now. They'll have moved on. I know the drill. Dozens of new, fresh-faced little girls will have clamored to take my place, and they will all have been able to do my part just as well as I was. I guess I've always been replaceable. I'm nothing special, and that's all there is to it. It's just a fact.

> (ELLA adjusts CLARA on her shoulder and walks towards the window of the bedroom.)

So, here we are, little one. Neither of us is going anywhere. Let's dry our tears. No point in crying. Things are as they are, and goodness knows we can't change them. There. No more crying. C'mon baby girl, let's go watch the rain. It's so pretty, today. Look at the way it splashes on the windows. Look at that, little one. And do you hear the thunder? It's so loud! Mama loves the thunder. I think you do, too, pumpkin. Look at that smile! Look at you smile.

> (A phone rings.)

Huh. Who do you think is calling us, pumpkin? Who's calling Mama and Clara?

> (ELLA walks over to the dresser and picks up a cell phone. She looks at the screen and sighs.)

Would you look at that, baby girl? It's Grandma. Should we answer?

CLARA
Mmmmmmm, mmmmmmma.

ELLA
I'm afraid you're probably right, little one.

> (ELLA taps a button on her phone. SHERRY appears in her own home onstage. SHERRY is also talking into a phone.)

SHERRY
Ella! Finally! I've been trying to get ahold of you all morning. I have the most wonderful news. Where are you? Can you talk? Oh, never mind; I can't wait any longer to tell you. I have just found a wonderful job for you. It's perfect, simply perfect.

ELLA
Wow, Mom. It was so nice of you to think of me, but I'm not looking for—

SHERRY
You can thank me later, darling. Now, listen to this: the prep school downtown is looking for a dance teacher! Do you know the one I'm talking about? It's that high school that always has those poor girls wearing the most atrocious ties. St. Catherine's, I think it's called. How else can I describe it? It's this big, gray building with little eagles carved into its entrance and... You don't remember it, do you? It's been so long since you visited home...

ELLA

Mom, I remember St. Catherine's and it's great that they're hiring. But I can't apply for that job. I live here now, in Chicago, and you and that school are all the way up in Michigan. Andy will never want to move; you know that. Besides, that school has their teachers working at all hours. I'd always be teaching, and Clara's still so little. I can't leave her, not yet.

SHERRY

Don't be ridiculous, Ella. I thought you wanted to dance again. Haven't you been moping about not being able to since Clara was born? Here's your chance to get back to ballet. My sources tell me that the post is quite prestigious and very technical. You would teach actual ballet to competent students, not twirls to three-year-olds. I know it's not quite what you wanted, I know it's not the stage, but the pay is good, and you might find that you love teaching. I'd be happy to watch Clara for you, if that's what it takes for you to feel comfortable. Your father and I want to see more of your sweet baby anyway. We could help you move too! It would be a quick job; you haven't got many things, just a few boxes of your clothes and of Clara's toys.

ELLA

Mom, I can't move. I really can't. Andy has his work here; our lives are here. I can't just uproot my family.

SHERRY

I don't see why. Really, you haven't given me one good reason why you and Clara couldn't live a bit closer. Michigan has so much to offer: a job for you, grandparents for Clara, and... Well, I suppose your husband doesn't gain anything from moving. But that man gets everything he wants. No one tells him no, and it goes to his head. Andy has such an inflated sense of self-importance, Ella. I really don't see how you put up with him. I, personally, can't stand listening to him drone on about that startup of his for more than five minutes. How can any man be so in love with himself? If Andy doesn't want to come to Michigan, maybe you should just leave him in Chicago. It'd be no loss. I mean, really, he's always so... absent. From your life and from Clara's. Wouldn't it be easier to leave all your loneliness behind in Chicago?

ELLA

I'm not leaving Andy, if that's what you're suggesting.

SHERRY (Sighing)

Why?

ELLA

I am married to Andy. I married him two years ago in a tiny church near his parents' house. You were there, remember?

SHERRY (Impatiently)

I know that, Ella. I wouldn't complain about Andy half as much if he wasn't related to us. But I don't see your point.

ELLA

My point is he's my husband. And Clara's father. To leave would be to give up on all that. Clara and I would be alone. If I left...

SHERRY

You'd be happier.

ELLA

I'm not sure that I would, Mom. I'm not sure it's that simple.

SHERRY

Well, obviously I'm not saying that moving would be *simple*, but you always sound so miserable when you call. Honey, I just want what's best for you. And I think home is what you need right now.

ELLA

But I'm not sure that I want—

SHERRY

Come home, Ella. Take the job. Let me help you.

(CLARA begins to cry loudly. Neither SHERRY nor ELLA speaks for a minute.)

ELLA (Softly)

Clara's hungry. I'll call you tomorrow, okay?

SHERRY

Fine. But think about what I said, Ella. Bye, now.

(SHERRY hangs up the phone. SHERRY and her home disappear from view. ELLA moves toward the door of the bedroom, still carrying CLARA, who has quieted.)

ELLA

Well, what do you think, baby girl? Do you want to live in Michigan? You've never been, I know. But maybe we could use a change. And you'd like it there; I'm sure you would.

(Scene ends.)

Scene 2

AT RISE: The kitchen of the apartment at night. ELLA sits at a table. ANDY enters the room and ELLA stands to greet him.

ANDY

Ella, you're still up. Wow, late night for you, huh? It's like ten. Where's Clara?

ELLA

She's sleeping. She's been in bed since about seven.

ANDY

Well, good for you, I guess. It's nice that you got some free time, tonight. Doesn't seem like you've had much since Clara was born.

ELLA

I was actually a bit lonely after she fell asleep. I've gotten so used to having her with me. She's nice to talk to.

ANDY

And I'm sure that the pair of you must have fascinating conversations. Anyway, I'm off to bed, so...

ELLA

My mom called today.

ANDY

Did she?

ELLA

Yes, Andy, she did.

>   (Andy sighs. He sits on kitchen chair and tips it onto its hind legs. ELLA remains standing.)

ANDY

Okay, I'll bite. What did Sherry have to say? Wait, I'll guess. Ummm, she wants to move in with us because your dad's driving her crazy. No, no... She's flying to Guatemala to teach ballet to under-privileged children and insists that you come along. No... Hold on, I've got it. She's sure that I can't possibly be Clara's father, and demands that you get a paternity test. Sherry says that I'm really much too awful to be related to your daughter and... Ella, you're not smiling. That's not what your mom wanted, is it?

ELLA

Andy, my mom wants me to move back to Michigan. There's this job that she heard about. A school in her town needs a dance teacher and—

ANDY

Ella, you don't need to work. Really, my job at the startup more than allows you to stay home with Clara. Money is not an issue.

ELLA

I know, and it's not the money. I just... miss dancing. I miss it like crazy. Ballet was such a big part of me for years and years... I feel sort of empty without it.

ANDY

Ella, honey, if you miss ballet so much, just go take an adult dance class. They have them down at the community center. I'm sure we could get a baby-sitter to come in for one night a week. Clara would be fine, and it would be good for you to reconnect with your old pastime. You've seemed so withdrawn lately. Kind of depressed, honestly. Maybe you should go see your doctor, too. He might be able to prescribe some pills to, ah, lift your spirits.

ELLA

You don't get it, do you? Dancing isn't my hobby, Andy. It was my entire life before Clara. Now, I can't even play *The Nutcracker* without you making me shut it off. Ballet has been totally stamped out of my life; of course, I seem depressed. Those dance classes at the center aren't going to do a thing for me, either. I know what they're like. They're taught by a teacher who knows nothing about ballet, and they are made for first-time dancers. I have been a ballerina for twenty years, Andy. I am hardly a beginner.

> (ANDY returns the chair's legs to the floor. He stands and walks toward ELLA.)

ANDY

Whoa, Ella. I'm not suggesting that you are. Deep breaths, okay. You're going kind of ballistic on me and it's just because you're tired. Come on, let's get you to bed and we can talk more in the morning.

ELLA

I want to talk about this now, Andy. We need to talk now. Please. You won't be here tomorrow. You're never here.

ANDY
I really don't see what there is to say, Ella. Once you've rested, you'll see that everything is fine. You've got a safe home, a healthy baby, and a husband who loves you: pretty much everything a person could want. It's all okay.

ELLA
No. No, it's not. It's not okay. None of this is okay.

ANDY
Look, Ella, I'm sorry life hasn't turned out like you wanted it to. I'm sorry that your career never took off. I'm sorry that you had Clara. All right? I'm really sorry. Is that what you wanted to hear?

ELLA
I'm never sorry that Clara was born. Never.

ANDY
Okay... great then. Everything's good. Can we go to bed now?

ELLA
I'm not sorry that Clara was born, and I don't regret giving up the stage for her. I will never regret that. But something is still missing inside of me. I have a hole in who I am and no idea how to fill it. I'm not a ballerina anymore, so who am I? Clara's mom, Andy's wife, Sherry's daughter, sure, but those are roles, not identities. I don't have a clue who Ella is. Maybe going home would help me figure it out. Maybe going alone would give me more space to.

ANDY
Aww, come on, Ella. Don't be dramatic. You just need—

>(Off-stage, CLARA cries. ELLA walks in the direction of the cries.)

ELLA
That's Clara. You can go to bed. My baby needs me.

>(Scene ends.)

Scene 3

AT RISE: It is the next morning in the kitchen, and a light rain raps on the kitchen window. CLARA sits in a swing while ELLA washes dishes.

ELLA

Would you look at that: it's still raining. Mama loves the rain, baby girl, but some sun would be nice.

(ELLA stops washing dishes and walks over to CLARA's swing. ELLA sits down in a chair beside it.)

I have some news, pumpkin. Grandma called again this morning, way before you woke up. Do you know what she said? Well, poor Grandma called to tell us that the job at St. Catherine's filled a bit quicker than she had been expecting. There really is no point in us thinking of moving to Michigan now; Grandma and Grandpa can't support us if I'm not working. Our chance to go home is gone, baby girl.

CLARA

Bleh, bleh.

ELLA

Yep, sweetheart, I feel yucky too. But I don't really think that Michigan would have made us feel any better. And as lonely as we are here, I'm not ready to be alone. We still need your daddy, no matter what Grandma says. We need him in your life. So, I guess I'm just going to have to soul-search in Chicago, though I have no idea what it is that I'm looking for. What do you think, Clara? Who can Mama be now? I suppose you and I will have to find out together.

CLARA

Mmmmmmm-mmmmmma.

ELLA
I'm glad that you agree, little one.
> (ELLA stands and lifts CLARA out of her swing.)

Well, what shall we do? We've got nothing but time, you and me. You know what? I have an idea.
> (ELLA pushes the kitchen chairs away from the center of the kitchen and turns on the radio. We hear classical music.)

What do you think Clara? Do you like the music? I love it. I really, really do. And it's great for dancing. So, what do you say? Do you want to dance with me, pumpkin? Because I'd love to dance with you. Ready? Here we go.
> (ELLA and CLARA slowly dance around the kitchen, spinning in circles.)

What do you think, baby girl? Is this fun? You're smiling like it is. Should we try going faster?
> (ELLA speeds up slightly, and CLARA begins to giggle.)

Listen to that laugh. It's such a beautiful laugh.
> (They continue to dance.)

I love it when you're happy, Clara. It makes me feel like I did when I danced beside prima ballerinas. I knew that no one in the audience would look away from them and see me, but just being in their presence felt meaningful. That's like you, sweet pea. You are the center of my world; the spotlight is trained upon your beautiful little face. And I'm always going to be here, in the background.

> (Scene ends.)
> (End of Play.)

Hannah Gregory, 11th Grade
St. Mary's High School

THE THANKLESS MAYOR
by Jonathan Gregory

CAST OF CHARACTERS

ELIZABETH   Executive assistant to the mayor. She is dissatisfied with her job but is still fond of INDIANA.

INDIANA   The well-meaning mayor. Is disheartened by resistance to his policies, despite putting on a cheery façade.

ANDREA   Director of the city's Center for the Arts. Is extremely critical of the mayor's policies.

MAN   Music teacher.

Scene
The mayoral office in the City Hall of a small city.
A park in the city.

Time
A Wednesday, present time.

Scene 1

AT RISE: The mayor's office sits on the second floor of the town hall on Main Street, just above a municipal court.

Inside, ELIZABETH sits at a desk, talking on the phone to her sister while examining a large pile of paperwork labeled "incoming."

It is one o'clock, and all in the government building are returning to work after lunch.

ELIZABETH (On the phone)
Oh, that break does not do my job justice! Waking up at seven to catch the bus, working from nine to six, only to get a measly thirty minutes off? I should have listened to you, Sherry; I should have stuck with that job at the bank. No, Indiana's not over-working me. Well, I guess he is, but not intentionally. There's just not a lot of appreciation for my work, you know? A little "thanks" or "great job" would be nice once in a while. Ah, well, I can hear the elevator coming up. Talk to you later? All right, love you, sis. Bye.

(The elevator dings and the doors open. The mayor, INDIANA, walks into the office.)

INDIANA (Sing-song)
Afternoon, Elizabeth.

ELIZABETH (Sighing)
Hello, sir.

INDIANA
I know that sigh. What's got you down?

(ELIZABETH gestures at the mountain of paperwork on the desk)

ELIZABETH
Care to take a guess?

INDIANA

Oh, that's just a little pile. Remember that load we had last spring? I didn't get a wink of sleep for nearly two days!

ELIZABETH (Muttering)

I didn't sleep for three.

INDIANA

Cheer up, Lizzie! It'll be all right. See? I'll take half.

(INDIANA picks up half of the pile.)

All this work is worth it. You've just got to remember our goal, our mission.

ELIZABETH

I've already forgotten.

INDIANA

Let me illuminate, then. The city, before us, was ... in need of improvement, to put it mildly. Well, after just a year, we've turned things around. We have encouraged business; we've elevated the infrastructure; and we've beautified parts of the city. All with a limited budget. Imagine what we could do with a bigger one!

ELIZABETH

Have you seen our funds lately? We can barely buy a pack of staples, much less finance a total facelift on the whole city.

INDIANA

Yes, and that's why I've put together a little something in this year's budget. First, where do you get funds? From taxpayers. And where do you find taxpayers? In houses and stores and restaurants. Except no one wants to live or shop or eat here because city life is still not quite up to par for those suburbanites. So here it is, my plan to fill our coffers: we revitalize the downtown, put in some fine apartments and businesses. A better downtown equals more taxpayers; more taxpayers equal more money for the city. What do you think? Exciting stuff, right?

ELIZABETH
Wow. That's... an ambitious plan. Have you talked to anyone else about it?

INDIANA
I mentioned it to the council. They shot it down, like they do all new ideas. They still work by candlelight, those luddites. I think I can scrape together enough for a pilot project, though, just to show them that it can work.

ELIZABETH
Where is this money coming from?

INDIANA
Just a little siphoned here and there, mostly from tedious community renovation projects. If all goes well, the returns should balance the budget perfectly.

ELIZABETH
And if all does not go well?

INDIANA
Then I guess the city can make do without some non-essentials. We'll still have firemen and the police; we might just have to shelve some culture projects, like the City Center for the Arts restructuring project. This plan of mine is, after all, more important.

ELIZABETH
I don't know about this—

INDIANA (Interrupting)
Oh, the ends justify the means, Elizabeth. Just you see; this endeavor will be the crowning achievement of our administration. In the meantime, what's on the docket?

ELIZABETH
You've got to plan your visit to the elementary school, call Commissioner Lewis, and sign a few forms concerning the maintenance contract for the park. Plus, the papers you're holding.

INDIANA
Great. I'll take those in my office.
>(INDIANA walks into his part of the partitioned office. As ELIZABETH begins to sort through the papers on her desk, the elevator dings and the doors open. Out steps ANDREA.)

ANDREA (Muttering angrily)
Where is that man?

ELIZABETH
Oh, hi Andrea. Do you have an appointment here?
>(ANDREA pushes past ELIZABETH's desk and storms into the mayor's portion of the office, with ELIZABETH close behind her.)

Wait! You can't just barge in there without invitation! Sorry sir, she just walked in. Do you want me to call security?

INDIANA
No, no, that won't be necessary. I always have time for "concerned citizens" to tell me everything that I'm doing wrong. To what do I owe the pleasure, Andrea?

ANDREA
Oh, this will be no pleasure for you, "sir." I heard about your plan, and what it'll do to the city. How could you?

INDIANA
How could I what? And how did you learn about that?

ANDREA
Commissioner Lewis let it slip. What are you thinking, putting

the Center for the Arts at risk with your budget cuts? If you want to squander funds on this little construction project of yours, that's your business. But leave my Center out of it!

INDIANA

Ms. Andrea, I hardly think that a reallocation of funds puts the Center at any real risk.

ANDREA

That's not what the commissioner said. Do you understand how much hinges on the Center for the Arts in this town, Mr. Mayor? The Center must be funded!

INDIANA

Climb off your high horse, Ms. Andrea, and look around you. The city is near-empty, and I'm trying to fill it. If that means exchanging concert halls for condominiums, so be it. I appreciate your mission, but my administration currently values the downtown's revitalization more than it does the Center for the Arts.

ANDREA

Mr. Mayor, this is an argument of more importance than you give it. The Center for the Arts is musical education for children; it is the place kids go to learn about art, music, and theater, now that the council has cut those from the schools. The Center is the last place in the city anyone can get an education in the arts. It's not just a building; it's a destination. Surely, you can't cast this aside in favor of a few concrete monstrosities.

INDIANA

Surely, I can. I took an oath to serve this city, and I intend to do as I deem fit.

ANDREA

You think that you actually help the city? By cutting funding to public programs, by treading on public will?

INDIANA

The public is interested in keeping the streets clean and business booming, and I am doing my best. Now, if you please, I have more of the city to help.

ANDREA

As if you have made a difference!

> (The two speak at the same time, not listening to the other.)

ANDREA	INDIANA
I don't understand it. You cannot decimate an entire cultural program and continue personal insults cannot discredit that! I'm sorry, but this petty behavior quite illustrates why the drama in this town is getting downsized!	This is getting out of hand. What I have done has yielded visible marks of progress, and to think that you are helping the city to flourish. Frankly, your project is a waste, and until you work to help the city, your policies will continue to stagnate.

> (A loud noise from the street of trash being dumped, startling both ANDREA and INDIANA into a momentary silence.)

INDIANA

Enough. It is clear that this is going nowhere. Elizabeth, would you please show our visitor to the door?

ELIZABETH

Sure. Come on, Andrea. This way, please.

ANDREA

I meant what I said! If you won't reconsider your budget, perhaps you should reconsider your place in this office. Good day!

> (ANDREA exits in a huff. INDIANA looks agitated.)

INDIANA

What an insufferable person! The nerve, to walk in here and tell me that I'm a waste? Darn lack of propriety, that's what it is.

> (ELIZABETH and INDIANA both return to work at their desks. After a minute, INDIANA walks out of his partitioned office.)

Lizzie, you ... you don't think that she had any truth in what she said, do you?

> (Elizabeth is not paying attention.)

Elizabeth.

ELIZABETH (Exasperated)

What?

INDIANA

I asked you if you thought that Andrea was right about what she said.

ELIZABETH

Well, you are hitting the Art Center kind of hard with those cuts. I mean, the city has always supported the fine arts. And we did promise the Center those funds.

INDIANA

That's all well and good, but things are different now than they were then. There have been recessions and crashes; the city needs be helped back up to its feet, and I'm the one to do it. I accept that my plan isn't perfect, but it can help. But not if it's put in conflict with a program that has nothing to do with my mission goals.

ELIZABETH

Your mission goals? What has gotten into you, sir? You're sounding brash and inconsiderate, and—

> (The landline rings.)

                   INDIANA

I will do what I must to help the city; if that means opposing the council, even you, I will do it.

                   ELIZABETH

What do you mean?

    (INDIANA exits the office.)

Hey, where are you going? Sir!

        (Scene ends.)

SCENE 2

    AT RISE: A city park, small but well-maintained.

    INDIANA is sitting alone on a park bench. He looks tired and anxious and is quietly talking to himself.

                   INDIANA (To himself)

What's gotten into me, she says. Ha! What's gotten into her, more like. What's gotten into all of them? Elizabeth, the council, Andrea; if they could only see how necessary this plan is to keep the city afloat. We need growth and urban renewal; a newer Center for the Arts can't do that; there's just no way. They're too inflexible; that's the problem! But even Elizabeth is against me. How could she? Arghh!

    (With the last word, INDIANA throws up his hands violently. A man walking through the park notices INDIANA's outburst and walks up to him.)

                   MAN

Hey, buddy, are you all right? You look a little rattled.

                   INDIANA

Oh, yeah, pardon me. A hard day at work, you know?

MAN

Tell me about it. I heard just today that I might get laid off in a bit, so I get where you're coming from. Hey, have we met before?

INDIANA

No, no. I've just got one of those faces. That's a crummy bit of news you got. Where do you work?

MAN

I run the musical education at the Art Center down the road. You wanna hear some intel? The mayor wants to cut our funding. That's why I'm gonna lose my job. Now, I don't wish to trash the guy—he has made this park a bit safer, but this is a bit of a rotten deal. Sure, a lot of money promised to the Center was going toward renovations—new equipment and the like—but it was also going to pay me and a lot of others. It's not like we can get extra jobs; we each invest all our time in keeping the Center afloat.

INDIANA

Well, I'm sure he's got his reasons. What do you guys do down there at the Center, anyway? It never seems all that busy.

MAN

Well, you've clearly never been there Friday nights. We host a little community arts showcase, and the place is packed. People will take any chance they get to make a night of the city. They might go to the new restaurant downtown, maybe stop for a stroll around the park, and then head down to the Center. I mean, we see everyone, even people who have long since moved out to the 'burbs. There's a lot more money moving around here. It's breathing a little more life into the city.

INDIANA

Is that so? I've never heard of that before. But that's just Friday. What about the rest of the week? What about tonight?

                          MAN

You've got a lot of questions, buddy. Why don't you just check it out for yourself? I'm walking to the open house now. You might as well make use of the Center while it's still staffed, right?

                        INDIANA

Well, I've got to ... Oh, why not? Is it just down this way?

                          MAN

Yup. Just follow me.

> (The MAN leads INDIANA down the path in the park, toward the Center for the Arts.)

> (Scene ends.)

SCENE 3

> AT RISE: The mayoral office on Main Street. It is 7 p.m.
>
> ELIZABETH is still working on paperwork when INDIANA enters. There is a large stack of paperwork on her desk, now labeled "outgoing".
>
> (The elevator dings and the doors open. Out steps INDIANA, looking invigorated.)

                        INDIANA

Well Elizabeth, I've got some news.

                       ELIZABETH

Hopefully it's good.

                        INDIANA

Well, both good and bad, depending on the view. First, I've had a deep and insightful talk with a focus group, and I've determined that the Center for the Arts is much too valuable to lose. I'll work to secure its funding.

ELIZABETH
Well, I'm glad you came to your senses. That is very good news.

INDIANA
However, my downtown revitalization project, is still moving forward. I figure just because we do a bit of urban development doesn't mean we have to abandon the local interest, right? The two complement each other.

ELIZABETH
Exactly. That's what I was trying to tell you earlier: find a happy medium.

INDIANA
Hmm. It didn't really sound like that. I forgive you, though, for doubting me and my plans. It happens, I suppose.

ELIZABETH
Sir, nobody, except for maybe Andrea, was doubting the validity of you or your proposal. Certainly, I wasn't.

INDIANA
Sure, you did. Remember? "Your plan is inconsiderate" and all that.

ELIZABETH
Goodness gracious, I was talking about your plan to defund the Art Center, not the urban rehabilitation project!

INDIANA
You say that now, but I read between the lines earlier. I get that we don't agree on policy as much now as we once did, but I really count on your support. To lose the trust and backing of my second-in-command, my advisor, was… shaking, to say the least.

ELIZABTEH
Listen, I trust you; I think you're a good man, with good ideas. And while I might not always rejoice in your policies, I'm still

with you, all the way. You've got a decent plan. It needs a little refining, though. You can't hinge the city's funds on a single project, and that is where Andrea has a point. Let's not leap before looking into this. We'll go through the process, hammer out a few proposals, and get this done properly. In the meantime, please negotiate with Andrea before she organizes a mob.

INDIANA (Sheepish)

Oh, wow. I didn't know you felt like that. I'll get to work then. I... uh... I'm sorry I stormed out and left you to do all the work.

ELIZABETH

Forget about it. You're doing as best as you're able. I didn't do your paperwork for you, though, nor do I plan to.

INDIANA

Right, right. That paperwork. I'll get to that after I call Andrea. How about you take the rest of the night off? You certainly deserve a break. I can close up.

ELIZABETH

No, no. I'll stick with you here.

INDIANA

I know I haven't said this enough, but... thanks. We both know you're the stable one in this office. Without your support, I'd probably suffocate in this swamp of paperwork. Thanks for helping me out.

ELIZABETH

I know you'd do the same for me.

INDIANA (Clears throat)

Well, wish me luck with Andrea.

> (INDIANA walks into his part of the office, leaving the door open. He calls ANDREA, periodically moving the receiver from his ear when the volume gets too high.)

Hello Andrea. This is Mayor Indiana. No, no, no; there's no need for that language. Hey! This is a peace deal. I've got a compromise, if you'll hear it. No, no tricks. Well, I talked to one of your employees, and went to one of your open houses. You've got some interesting stuff going on there, and ...

(INDIANA's voice fades.)

(Scene ends.)
(End of Play.)

Jonathan Gregory, 11th Grade
St. Mary's High School

TANGO OF LOVE
by Mathew Hosler Jr.

CAST OF CHARACTERS

DIEGO   DIEGO is a young adult, around 25.

He is a hopeless romantic. He's dressed in a black suit with a red tie. He's thin and acts as though he's a confident person, when truthfully, he is not.

MARIANA   MARIANA is a young woman, around 20. She wears a beautiful black and red dress. She wears sparkling black and red make-up. She is thin, and shorter than DIEGO. She and DIEGO are in love. She doesn't move unless DIEGO is touching her.

GIRL DANCER   This character wears various shades of blue in make-up and her dress. She has no lines, and solely dances with DIEGO. She doesn't move unless DIEGO is touching her. Shorter than DIEGO.

BOY DANCER   This character wears a black suit, and a green shirt. He has no lines, and solely dances with DIEGO. He doesn't move unless DIEGO is touching him. He is somewhat shorter than DIEGO.

Scene
Within the mind of DIEGO as he desperately tries to find love.

Note
The director may choose the music he or she considers the best fit for the play. The playwright's preference would be tango music.

Scene One

AT RISE: Two characters stand on the stage.
Neither move nor speak. One man, one woman. Another man, DIEGO enters stage left. He walks to the center of the stage between the two others. He stands still for a moment. The stage is very dim, and very silent. He looks slowly at one person, then the other.

DIEGO

Welcome to my mind, you beautiful creatures. You both remain still, for I have yet to grab your attention. But do not worry, I will come to you when I am ready. Diego knows what he wants. And I want you. Both of you.

> (He approaches the woman, and as soon as he touches her, she begins to move. They hold one another close, on the verge of kissing. The tango music begins to play, quietly.)

DIEGO

You are so beautiful.

> (They begin to dance to the music.)

Yes. Wonderful dancing. Oh, I love you more than life itself. I will never leave you.

> (He lifts her off the ground and spins before lowering her back to her feet. They never lose one another's touch.)

Don't you just love the way we work together. It's magical, isn't it?

> (All lights go off except a spotlight on the two
> of them. It follows them as they dance. Their dance
> intensifies.)

Yes! I have clearly picked the right partner. You are amazing at what you do.

> (Pause)

Sweet lady, where are you from. It must be the heavens, for only an angel could look and dance the way you do. Oh, lay a kiss on my lips so I may feel the sensation of lust that I know you feel for me. So that my heart may begin to ache in pain as we hold one another. So that, as we dance, we may rub our bodies against one another and melt in the warmth of our love.

> (He pulls her close. They hold one another very
> tightly before he spins her away. She freezes in
> place as soon as he stops touching her. The music
> stops. He speaks to the audience.)

The fun in that was not enough. There was no emotion. There was no longing to be together. She danced with me, not in a romantic way, but in the way of pure lust. I wish for connection. I wish for unconditional love. For vows, and family. For a house which sits alone on an island, where we can swim naked in the ocean, and make love in the sand. I wish... I wish for happiness! And yet, when I danced with her, I felt nothing. I felt nothing but a desire to kiss. A desire to dance beneath the sheets of a bed. But is love not more than that? Is love nothing but sex with one person forever? That can't be it. There has to be something I'm missing. There has to be more to love than just happy pants. But what is it?

> (The song restarts, and he rushes to the other man, pull
> ing him close.)

You seem very powerful. Of course, you should know now that I don't let people push me around. Don't worry, I'll take the lead. You just try to keep up.

> (They begin to dance, almost fighting over who leads the
> entire time.)

Interesting. You want so badly to take the lead, but you need to understand...

> (He pulls the man directly against him, chest to chest, as he whispers into his ear.)

I don't share the spotlight.

> (They continue to dance.)

There you go. Yes, give in to me. Let me show you the new order of things. Let me show you a life of utmost prosperity, and beauty. What a marvelous thing love is. You make my stomach knot, as though I am to vomit, and yet I don't. I just keep dancing, and it's magnificent.

> (Pause)

Teach me the way of your dance, and I shall teach you mine. Let us understand one another's bodies, so that we may understand how to please each other. There are few things I desire, but I refuse to be without them. Late nights watching movies, or painting. Coming home from work and smiling at the sight of you. Comforting my lips with your glorious forehead. Yet most of all, holding you close to me every night as we sleep. The warmth of your body doing more for me than any blanket in the world.

> (The man slowly slides down the front of DIEGO, who instantly pulls him back up.)

No. Our dance will stay like this. We will continue to move with one another in ways I see fitting. And you will love it.

> (They continue to dance.)

Tell me about yourself. What do you long for in life? Where are you from? Where do you work? Do you have any pets? What are you passionate about underneath that thick skin of yours? Where do you want to go? Tell me anything about yourself. No, wait. Don't tell me anything. I don't want to ruin this moment of pure grace. This moment of... joy... Or do you not feel it? Don't answer that. Why are you so difficult to work with? You constantly fight for dominance in our dance, and you seem interested only in my body. You haven't asked me any questions, and you haven't shown any interest in my mind. You confuse me. This dance is more than just a dance. This dance is... is life. This dance is everything I look for, and everything I fight so hard to keep. This dance is me. This dance is my loved one. This dance is... this dance is...

> (DIEGO pulls the man close and their lips nearly connect before DIEGO spins the man away. The man freezes in place. The music stops.)

This dance is not for you...

> (Pause)

Maybe I'm not meant for love... Maybe... maybe I'm meant to be alone forever...

> (The stage goes dark. The other two exit when they're not visible. Spotlight on DIEGO as he sits on the ground, his hands in his lap.)

Maybe the world isn't as grand as I thought. Maybe I'm destined to die alone and hold nobody in my arms at night. Destined to cry each night and ponder what I have done to deserve the god's punishment. Ponder what vile deed I have done, and to whom it was done. I can't... I can't imagine what it must've taken... What must've happened to result in my loss of love? I don't want to be alone...

> (Begins to cry as he pulls a revolver from behind him.)

I... I can't be alone. Love is... love is oxygen. To hell with gravity. Love ties us to this planet. Love is the sun, which brightens each day with its warmth. It's the moon which lightens our dark and cruel world each night. Love is... is wings. Wings that lift us from our sorry lives to something more glorious. Something addictive and free. And if I am to live each day, watching the world around me find happiness, then I would sooner choose not to live. If it is greed that I feel, then I don't care. Everyone deserves love. To love somebody and be loved in return. To cry upon a shoulder when sadness is too much, and to comfort when they feel the same. It doesn't matter who is being loved. Everyone needs it. And I... I... I...

> (Pause)

I can't bear to live without it...

> (He slowly raises the revolver to his head, crying as he touches the trigger.)

Do it! You weak fool! Do it now! End your pathetic and miserable life! Do something right for a change! Remove yourself so that the world may never have to see you again! So that no man or woman has to turn you down when you seek their love! You are worthless!

> (Through his whimpers, he slowly begins to scream louder and louder before throwing the gun aside and sobbing as he falls to the floor.)

Even now... even now when you know you're destined to live your life alone every day, you're too much of a coward to end yourself. There is no doubt anymore of why you won't find love. You are too pathetic. You're too much of a pussy to take charge of the situation. Too weak to finish yourself. How can you ever hope to find love if you can't even control yourself? How can you hope to be happy if you can't even do the one thing everyone wants you to do? You are pathetic. You are a weak, worthless piece of sh—! Shoot yourself! Do it!

> (Pause)

Why can't I do it? Wh-why can't I just make it all go away? All of the sadness and loneliness. All of the misery that I must endure each and every day. I could stop it all. I could make it all go away forever. But I can't. I grip the trigger, but can't. Maybe I am too weak.

> (Pause. He stops crying, rushes to the gun, grabs it and stands with it against his head)

No! No! I am not weak! I despise the weak! I am strong! Stronger now than ever before! I will no longer cry! I will pull myself up and do it! I will do it before my heart is broken again! Before all of my confidence is ripped away, and nothing but a frail skeleton remains! I will purge the world of my wretched misery! And maybe in the afterlife I will find love. So now I go.

> (Pause)

Goodbye.

> (There is a short pause as DIEGO exhales. The spotlight turns off. Stage lights slowly turn on, and MARIANA stands on the stage, well-dressed. DIEGO slowly lowers the gun before dropping it, and walking towards the girl.)

You... you are the most beautiful person in the world.

> (He slowly circles her, admiring her up and down.)

There is so much to you, my eyes will never grow bored looking at you. Your form, every curve of you, is unchallenged. You are ... you are a goddess of lust. You radiate a perfume that my nose cannot stop enjoying. Oh, please ... would you dance with me?

> (He takes her hand and the two begin to dance more gracefully than in the other dances.)

You are so great at this. You dance with the ferocity of a tiger, yet the grace of a fish. You are swift, and tough. You are...

MARIANA

I am Mariana.

> (The music pauses)

DIEGO

Mariana. You speak? You... You live... Never have I desired someone's attention more than now. Your name is as beautiful as the dress you wear. But nothing, I fear, can be more beautiful than your eyes, which I can't stop staring at, for they hold my universe within them.

MARIANA

And you... You are the handsome prince. I would sleep my life away if it meant you would be the one to wake me from the curse.

> (There is a pause, and the music begins again where it left off. They begin to dance immediately.)

MARIANA
You have quite a way with words, and you dance better than anyone I've ever met.

DIEGO
That's because, my dear, you have never met someone like me. Nor I you.

MARIANA
You haven't told me your name yet?

DIEGO
In all honesty, my love, I never usually get that far.

MARIANA
Should I fear what you might do then?

DIEGO
Mariana, my sweet... I would never give you a reason to fear me.

MARIANA
Then do one thing for me, stranger.

DIEGO
My name. Yes, I forgot to tell you my name. Diego, I am Diego. I would do anything, Mariana. Anything for you.

(MARIANA pulls him close, their noses touching.)

MARIANA
Kiss me.

(DIEGO spins her away and she freezes in place)

DIEGO
A kiss? She wants a kiss? Does she really love me? Or is she simply trying to lie with me like the others? Dearest Mariana, to kiss you would be to give in to you. To kiss you would be me letting you have whatever you want with me, when really I simply

long for you as a lover. I wish to make you my bride. To hug you and rest my hands on your stomach when you are with child. To please you no matter what, for you are a star that cannot burn out. I can't feel this way about you if you don't feel the same for me. I can't kiss you, because you may only want sex from me. I can provide that for you, but I cannot only provide that.

(Pause)

And if you want love... real love... and I leave, giving up on you... then we would both lose. I can't just go to you and let you break my heart, and yet in turn I cannot just leave and break yours. I must... be the man and see where you take me. I would rather my heart break, than yours. For I love you.

(He pulls her back in. There is silence as they stare at one another.)

MARIANA

Kiss me, Diego. I long for you. You are my everything, and I need you to feel the same for me. For if you don't, then I fear that you and I may never last. That all of my time spent with you was for nothing. If that is the case, Diego, tell me so that I may leave, and stop wasting my time here.

DIEGO

No, Mariana, that is not it at all. Words cannot describe how much I desire to kiss you, but I fear you will leave. I fear you will leave like everyone else who mattered to me. Like my father when I was young, and my mother when I was fifteen. I fear you will come and go like every other relationship in my life.

MARIANA

I would never, Diego. I would never leave you.

DIEGO

Mariana... I...

MARIANA

So, are you going to kiss me or not?

DIEGO
Mariana, to kiss you would be greater than life itself. But I cannot just kiss you. I want more than a kiss... I... I...

MARIANA	DIEGO
I love you.	I love you.

(Slowly the two draw into a kiss. Music begins, and they begin to dance.)

DIEGO
Never before have I met a person like you.

MARIANA
That's because, sweet boy, there is no person like me.

DIEGO
If there was ever a person like you, Mariana, I fear the world would have too many stars. For you are one of a kind.

MARIANA
If there was ever a person like you, Diego, I fear the world would be too lucky. For you are the one I've been looking for all of my life.

DIEGO
Sweet Mariana, at my lowest point, when I felt there was nothing left for me, you... you kept me going. You showed me my value, and you made me believe there was a life worth living. And there's only one thing left for me to do now.

MARIANA
What?

DIEGO
My dearest Mariana...

(The music stops as he kneels to one knee, holding her right hand.)

Will you live this life with me, and every life after it? Will you take my arm, and walk through the challenges of our future together? Will you, Mariana, take me as your husband, so that I may take you as my wife? So that I may endure the struggles of marriage with you at my side, and never falter? So that you and I may stand our ground at the gates of loneliness and tell the devil himself to get lost? Oh, Mariana, will you be mine? Will you be mine, and have me in return?

MARIANA

Diego, there is nothing I would want more than that.

    (He rises. They kiss once more.)

DIEGO

I love you Mariana... more than words can express.

MARIANA

Oh, Diego, there is no word to describe the amount of emotion I feel when I'm with you.

    (They hold one another close.)

MARIANA

Oh, Diego, I never want this moment to end. Can things just stay like this forever?

DIEGO

Only as long as you allow them to last, my dear.

MARIANA

Then I will never change this. I will let things stay like this forever. A simple fairy tale between a man and woman. A princess and her kind, handsome prince. A wish, a dream come true, and an unpredictable future. This, Diego, is our fairytale, which is something I didn't think I would ever truly have. And you have brought it to me. Oh, Diego, I love you so dearly. I can't begin to imagine what my life would be like without you in it. I want you to never leave me.

DIEGO
Then let us dance the tango of love.

    (The music begins. The two begin to dance. Lights slowly go off. The curtains fall.)

    (End Scene)
    (End Play)

Mathew Hosler Jr., 12th Grade
Kingsley High School

WELCOME
by Rebekah Keeder

"Welcome," said the soft voice of the artificial intelligence system made to look like a woman. "The exit is on your left. If you choose to exit, you may do so now but if you choose to stay, you will never get another opportunity to leave. You will spend the rest of your limited days here." Her voice never fluctuated. Never quivered or changed in pitch. The softness in "her" voice was both feminine and monotone, but the last few words seemed to bounce around him like little rubber balls connecting with the floor. They hit his ears, his vertebrae, and the inner walls of his brain sending shivers up and down his spine. Those words were cold enough to make the hair on his body stand on end; they created goose bumps and capsuled his insides in a thick coat of frozen honey. His blood ran cold. Peripheral vasoconstriction started with the tips of his fingers making them numb, then traveled to his feet which were now too cold to stand on. He couldn't get up, he couldn't leave; so, he stayed. With frozen bone marrow and blood that no longer reached his icy hands. He stayed.

"Welcome," said the same soft voice of the original artificial intelligence system made to look like a woman. "The exit is on your left. If you choose to exit, you may do so now, but if you choose to stay, you will never get another opportunity to leave. You will spend the rest of your limited days here." To her, those words had the same physical effects as a cow getting branded with a red-hot iron; the burning sensation radiated from her chest. "This brings a whole new meaning to heartburn," she thought to herself. This felt like hot metal traipsing down the bones in her back making it ache. Biting her ears was a fire-infused serrated blade, burning and stinging as if she was bitten, to the point where the wound needed to be cauterized. Her blood boiled so intensely it looked like maggots crawling underneath her now crimson skin, and her entire body dripped with a salty concoction of water and oils excreted by her human body.

"Interesting, is it not? Everybody seems to have a different reaction but these two in particular are experiencing the opposite feelings on a physical level, but their brain waves overlap with no outliers."

"You're right. How interesting, Professor. What do you suggest we do with this information? Should we run more tests on their brains after the drug wears off to see if they cope with the after-effects the same way? Or should we give them another dose before we scan their brains?"

"That's up to you, *Doctor*. What do you think we should be doing with these exquisite people? How does it feel to be called doctor, huh? We have been working with each other for thirteen years and you're calling me professor?

"I'm sorry, sir, I was just trying to—"

"Never mind what you were trying to do. Let's get back to the study so we can interview these participants and gather much-needed information."

"As you wish, sir."

"We just had this talk, Marley!"

They turned their attention back to the two people sitting in adjacent rooms, where they were finally coming down from the electronic high they had endured.

"Were you lucid enough to know what was happening during the process of us changing the chemicals in your brain with artificial intelligence, or did it feel real?" asked the professor.

"It felt real, but it also didn't evoke any form of pain. It's like when you dream and you fall but it doesn't affect you. You still felt that pain, though, just without physically feeling it. It was almost pleasant, I think? You knew it was there, but it wasn't painful, I guess would be the best way to describe it," replied George.

"Great, now would you please go into the next room on your right and wait for further instruction." George knew it wasn't really a question, so he complied.

"When we hooked you up to the artificial intelligence that we created to change the chemistry in your brain, were you lucid enough to know what was happening, or did you think that everything you were experiencing was real?" asked Dr. Marley.

"I knew that it wasn't reality, but I thought it was real at the same time. The weirdest part is that there was no actual pain, yet it hurt all the same. You could feel it as if it were happening to someone while you were watching but it never physically impacted you. It was almost as if the pain was completely empathetic, yet there was nothing to empathize with. I don't remember any physical pain, but I remember thinking that it should hurt. That it should burn. I don't really recall everything, but I remember being immensely surprised by what I felt because it wasn't painful," Lindsay said, trying to wrap her mind around the experience of feeling what should be painful—not to be numbed, but just not to be in pain.

"Wonderful, now I'm going to have you exit and enter the second door to your right. This interview has been useful."

When she arrived, she saw someone sitting in a white chair. Everything was white, well, everything other than the mirror that she knew had to be one-way glass. Why else would they have it here? The only bit of color was leaking from his navy-blue eyes. The white fabric she had to wear covered everything on her body but her eyes. It scratched at her skin and made her itch everywhere it touched. She thought it must've been made of wool because of how scratchy it was, but it was too light-weight for that to be the case.

"Hi, my name's George," he said while he was getting hooked up to the robot-like mechanism that altered their brain waves to induce an altered state of mind getting them "high" for the second time.

"Lindsay," she replied.

"So this is fun, huh?" said George.

"Oh yeah, I love getting hooked up to machinery just to make a little extra cash and to help out Big Pharma," was her retort.

"So, I guess you're just here for the cash?"

"Yeah, I'm running low on funds, and I saw an ad in the newspaper about getting money for getting high, and I thought it was a better idea than working the street corner."

"You're kidding, right?"

"No, I'm being one hundred percent serious about selling myself on a disgusting street-corner. Of course, I'm kidding!"

Once she was in place and hooked up to the "brain machine," they embarked on the second journey of what would soon be referred to as "A-High."

Rebekah Keeder, 12th Grade
TC West Senior High

3,926 MILE LOVE
by Camilla Kiessel

Layla chewed on the bubblegum-pink eraser that rested atop her yellow #2 pencil. A fresh piece of lined paper lay in front of her on a small wooden desk. Her legs were tucked close to her chest; her eyes, puffy and red from hours of crying, were staring blankly at the page. Why was this so hard? Why couldn't she just write out her emotions? Why couldn't she say how she felt? Oh right... Leon would never understand. He would never feel the same way. It was impossible to make it work and they both knew it. Yet, Layla was still there, she knew she just needed to release all these emotions, so with a deep shaky breath she touched her pencil to the paper and began to write.

Dear Leon,
How does one begin such a letter? With a simple hi, and how are you? Well I already texted that to you today. You're busy with exams, so I didn't want to bother you by typing this out and throwing it onto you. So, here I am, sitting at my desk and writing this letter to you. According to the post office it should get to you in a week, you'll be done with exams by then. You will also be home, away from your boarding school and stress, so this won't increase any stress... I hope. I feel like by now you probably know why I'm writing because why

else would I write instead of text you? I just want you to know that I don't expect you to do anything with this information. I just need to get these words, these feelings, out on paper. Okay... here it goes...

Layla's hand started to shake violently as she wrote three, simple words, *"I love you,"* on paper for the first time. She dropped her pencil and pushed herself away from the desk. Her breathing increased rapidly, and her heart was pounding in her chest. She closed her eyes, squeezing back the fat tears that threatened to run down her cheeks. After a few moments of silence, she opened her watery eyes to read what she had written.

"You can't just say it like that," Layla growled to herself as she shook her head in frustration and angrily erased the last sentence. With a deep sigh, she flipped her pencil over, touched the lead to the paper, and began to write once again.

It's almost by cruel fate that I met you. We were strangers, living miles apart. One year ago, was when you first messaged me, complimenting me on my artwork that I had been posting. I thanked you, thinking this was as far as it would go. But no, you asked if I could help you and of course I agreed. Flash forward two months; we had been talking every day since. I gave you my personal Instagram and you gave me yours. You were breathtaking in all your photos. Not long after, I was in a horrible state of mind, I was so close to ending it all. So close to leaving this cruel world. That's when my phone started buzzing, your name flashing across the screen. You were calling me. I quickly wiped away my tears and picked up. Immediately your French-accented voice filled my ears. I don't know how you did it, but you persuaded me out of making what would have been the worst and final decision of my life. How could I ever repay you? I can't and that's the problem. With the ocean and land between us, I cannot thank you with something as simple as a hug. Since that day, we enjoyed Skype that only ended when the sun began to rise over the grassy green hill that lies behind your house. It's been a year. A year of blissful friendship filled with laughter, tears, and all kinds of various emotions. We have met many new friends and also a few enemies. But whatever we went through, we went through it together. My problems were yours and your problems were mine. Then I started having these dreams. Dreams of you wrapping your arms around me, comforting and protecting me. Dreams of your soft lips on mine. Dreams of you whispering seductive words into my ear. Those dreams just confirmed the feeling that I had been trying to ignore by pushing it deep inside me whenever we talked. I had fallen for you. How could I not? You have those beautiful brown eyes that shine with intelligence and laughter. You have those brown messy curls that barely brush your collarbone. Your dazzling smile stands prominently against your clear, tan skin. You're my soulmate. I know you are. I can feel it in my heart, and I know you feel it too. I know because of your constant flirtatious texts and compliments. I know because the way you look at me is like no look I've ever seen. A look of love. You have all the physical and emotional attributes that I could ever imagine in a perfect partner. The only thing holding us apart, is the distance. 3,926 miles to be exact. And I know it could never work. We both need someone who can be there physically for us. We both need someone who would be able to drop everything, get in their car, and drive just to talk to us. I love you, Leo. More than you will ever know, and I want nothing more than to be with you, but it cannot happen. Maybe one day, when we grow old and we're traveling the world, we will run into each other at an airport. It would be a joyful reunion. But for now, I'm writing to you to say goodbye. I cannot keep talking to you every day, it makes

my feelings stronger when I need them to go away. I cannot pretend that I don't have these feelings anymore. I cannot continue as if nothing had happened. By the time you get this letter, you will have realized that I have removed you on all social media platforms. I'm sorry. My heart will throb and ache every day until maybe the day will come that you become a distant memory and maybe then, I will have the courage to send you a text. Until then, this is goodbye. I love you, Leon Roux.
Best Wishes,
Layla Wilson

A strangled sob escaped Layla's lips as she folded the letter and tucked it into a clean envelope. She grabbed her burgundy coat that was lined with brown fur. She pulled up the hood and pushed open the wooden door, the icy wind greeting her. It threatened to push her back inside, as if warning her that this letter was not meant to be sent out. But Layla fought back, continuing to push against the bitter, strong wind until she reached the little blue rectangular box on the side of the road. She hugged the letter close to her chest, her heart pounding at an unhealthy rate. Slowly, she pulled open the mail slot and slipped the letter through. She watched it as it twirled down and landed in the other piles of paper. Just one of many letters. The only difference? This letter will end something that never even had a chance to start.

Camilla Kiessel, 11th Grade
St. Francis High School

THE HOUSE MY GRANDPA BUILT
by Clara Kroll

Where over forty years ago there was a small field, now stands a house, white in color, a matching garage out back. In the well-kept yard stands a small group of trees, maybe eight trees or so, standing with their trunks and branches thick, arms extending outward and low enough that children could climb their branches—adults, too, if they tried. The trees hold memories of children now grown, and their children as well—days when they would swing from branches, build a makeshift badminton net, or fly off a wooden swing. In the front of the house, walking on the stone driveway, you'll notice the old basketball hoop, unused since my aunts moved out, and a tree growing right alongside the driveway, a small divot in its branches, where it once cradled a robin's nest. Inside the garage, attached to the house, there is the permanent smell of pipe tobacco, which has a sweetness to it that. In an odd sense, it always gave me a warm feeling as a child, reminding me of a plush carpet that absorbs me as I lay on it. In the kitchen of the house, one of the first rooms you see when walking in, there is no escaping the bright orange floors, a sheet of fake tiles that fittingly earned the nickname of the pizza floor, with varying circles and shades of orange that could only resemble pizza. The countertops used to be a dull orange as well, but my dad had long ago convinced my grandpa to replace them with white ones instead. At the end of one such counter, there is a tall swivel chair resting in front of a half wall, with rails extending into the ceiling, reminding me of the sides of long staircases. To more inventive, creative young children, they might be the bars of a jail cell. The living room carpet is in theme with the floors of the kitchen, matching the pizza floor with a slightly different shade of orange. The carpet, though, is much softer, kind of like wearing a pair of fuzzy socks, although you could only feel them every time your feet touched the floor. The fireplace at the back of the living room is solid stone, and once decorating the unused fireplace were pictures of his family—his four daughters, but mostly, his grandkids. The bedrooms where my mom and her sisters had slept contrasted in their own way; one was pure white, with simple dressers, the other white as well, but the dressers took up more space. The first room seemed brighter, and even though both rooms were the same color, the first had two windows, both of which let in the sun better than the single window bedroom on the other side of the wall. In both closets, there was tape marking the halfway point of their territory, some of the little evidence that sisters had shared those rooms. My grandpa's room was much darker, the change coming after his divorce with my grandma. At the foot of his bed, however, was a chest that had belonged to his mother, my namesake. The basement was much colder than the rest of the house, but when I was older, that didn't matter, since my brother, cousins, and I had discovered there was a pool table down there. It also held the army uniform he had worn so long ago, hanging from a pipe that ran across the ceiling.

 But when my grandpa moved out of that house, it was the memories and the life that he had lived there that he kept seeing over the course of those two days of moving. It had taken months for my mom to convince him that moving would be best, but still, my grandpa had been hesitant. Over the years, with my grandpa's growing back issues, the lawn had become unkempt, and he was struggling to keep up with the care of the house itself. Pictures on the fireplace had been coated with a thin layer of dust, dulling the shine of the golden frames, and the wooden ones seemed to gray with age.

My parents, one of my aunts, my brother, and I helped my grandpa move out of the house. Although memories weren't haunting me nearly as much as they were my grandpa, I would still look at the kitchen table, remembering the many games of Connect 4 that had been played there, the black and red circles bouncing off the table onto the floor, or the living room floor, where my grandpa had sat watching from the couch as my brother and I bickered over the rules of checkers and whether or not we'd just made a legal move, and where my brother and I had dumped the box of old toys—dump trucks, dominoes, trains, small toy cars and tractors, and stuffed animals –onto the carpet and our own, made-up little world.

For my grandpa, it was those memories, and the more than thirty years of memories that had come before it: building the house from the ground up with his former wife and oldest daughter after returning from Fort Benning, Georgia; the births of his other three daughters and watching all four of them grow up; the arguments with my grandma; standing with my grandma at their eldest daughter's wedding and the divorce that followed; my grandma and the younger three daughters packing their bags, leaving my grandpa alone; and my grandpa's regret over not being there more for his family in the house he had built for them all those years ago.

As he walked around the house when we were helping him pack, he dragged his feet, shuffling more than usual. Reminders of the memories were written all over his face, his eyes drifting to the now empty stone fireplace, where the pictures of all his family had once been. The more bare the house became, the slower he became. With every box carried out through the door to the garage, the sadder his face became, his eyes becoming duller, his mouth drooping down. As my grandpa watched my dad help load boxes into the moving truck, the pipe hanging from the corner of his mouth, the less he said.

I do remember that he became picky about what he kept, not being able to keep everything in the move to his new condo, and I remember that he did argue with my mom and aunt on a few things, my brother and I chiming in, especially when it came to the toys of our childhood. But with less room, as my mom told the three of us, there needed to be sacrifices. Grudgingly, we submitted to her requests.

As we moved things into the new condo as well, I remember my grandpa becoming picky about how the fridge was placed, becoming grumpier each time the fridge had to be shifted, or complaining about the new setup of his living room. Again, my mom reminded him, there were sacrifices; this wasn't going to be the same as his old house.

Standing in the new condo, at the mention of his house, my grandpa seemed to droop. We all knew that he loved that house, and still does, and even though he knew he couldn't stay in the house forever with his bad back, we could tell he missed it, even on that first day, when he wasn't even fully moved out. His life was at that house, with its memories of the children that once inhabited it, the many years he had spent with and without my grandma, and the new generation that gave the house new memories to hold.

With everything my mom, aunts, and grandpa have told me, I know my grandpa wasn't always there for his kids, having worked a lot, and interacted with his kids little, and he regrets not having done better. Never having been a fan of babies, my grandpa had a harder time connecting to kids. But when I was born, my mom, who had remained the closest to my grandpa throughout the years, was determined to change that. My mom forced my grandpa to hold me, showing him how to cradle my head in the crook of his arm, and how to gently place his hand so he was supporting me properly as he sat in his big blue Laz-Y-Boy. To say the least, my grandpa was freaked out, nervously cradling me in his arms, becoming more nervous as my mom walked to the kitchen to get my formula after determining my grandpa was doing perfectly fine holding me. My mom did the same thing with my brother a year or so later, forcing him into my grandpa's arms as I waddled around on the floor.

To me, it seemed like my mom literally pushing my brother and me into my grandpa's arms was a revelation for him. Maybe, not in that moment, or any specific moment, but over the course of time as my brother and I grew, my grandpa realized he had the opportunity so few get. "They're my second chance," he once told my mom. He wasn't planning on wasting it, and so far, he hasn't. My grandpa is an active part of both my life and my brother's, making it to at least one of our sporting events during the year, and if he can't, always asking about us. For me personally, he always asks about my piano lessons, and what I'm doing in my school's choir, what songs we're learning, what I'm practicing, and whenever he visits, he always wants to hear me play. There have been a few times where I've put the phone on speaker and played for him that way.

When my grandpa moved, my brother and I drove with him back and forth between his house and the condo. As he drove, at first the car was silent, except for the radio, my brother and I figuring out that my grandpa was just trying to seem okay in front of us; he didn't want us seeing how upset he really was. So instead, my brother and I made conversation, awkwardly, but we accomplished the task well enough. We talked about the most random of things: the weather, the road, our young lives, probably even the weeds growing in the ditches. My brother had long ago found the secret stash of candy that my grandpa keeps in his truck, and when we all got quiet again, my brother broke the silence by asking if he could eat the candy. "Only if you share," was my grandpa's response.

Change has never been easy for my grandpa. After my grandma left with his daughters, he didn't deal with it well at all. He doesn't talk about that time period much, but I do know that my mom stood with my grandpa, helping him get back on his feet and get back to living his life. I also know that if not for my mom, my grandpa may not have gotten his second chance to watch three of his daughters become the women they are today. Choosing to leave the house where he spent the majority of his life was not an easy change for him to accept either. In any conversation about the condo, he finds some way to tie in his house, even though it no longer belongs to him. There are some days in which he regrets the move entirely, but others in which he remembers that moving was better for his health.

Even though the house has stayed in the family, bought by one of my mom's cousins, it has changed a lot since my grandpa lived there. But to him, the house seems unchanged. Despite the fact that he now lives a couple towns over from where he used to live, my grandpa maintains the same love for the house and its memories, and the life he had lived there for almost half a century. He has a lot of pride in the house, as building a house from the ground up took a lot of saving and wasn't common in the small farming town of Posen. With all the life he's put into it, it remains his home, and always will.

Clara Kroll, 12th Grade
Glen Lake High School

THE ONE WHO CRIES IN THE BATHROOM AT A PARTY

by Clara Lick

A while back, I was invited to a party. You know, the big kind of party that is typically pivotal in a teenager's life, where there is dancing and drugs and making out behind closed doors. I can't say that I've never wanted that experience, because to say that would mean that I'm not a typical teenager. Back then, however, that was something I couldn't come to terms with. I was invited by a girl named Jess, who had dark green dyed hair and a punk rock attitude: the kind of confidence that shows in her stance, her walk, the way she talks. It's the kind of confidence that says, "I'll be myself, and I don't care if you like it or not." Some people would sell their soul to truly be like that (I can't deny that I would myself). Anyway, she awkwardly handed me an invite at my locker one day. This seemed weird because I know we've never talked outside of a schoolwork-related subject. She must've only invited me to be nice or something. When I got the invite, I kind of just stared at her, awe-struck. I never thought I'd even have the chance to go to a party like this in my whole life. I mean, I never really had friends after my best friend from sixth grade moved away, so this was a big chance for me to make some. Finally, in my junior year of high school, I could make some. I've never really been one for talking to people, but maybe Jess could introduce me to someone, and we could actually make conversation without me being awkward for once. Maybe we could exchange numbers when the party was over. Maybe we could text each other for hours on end, and maybe we could go get ice cream in the summer, and maybe we could comfort each other when we were feeling down, and if they went to a different school or something, I might finally be okay with sitting alone at lunch because I'd know that there was someone out there who liked me. A friendship like that would be worth more to me than anything else, more to me than any chance of teenage rebellion or experience that I would have at that party.

But it was all just some illusion, some hope of something that would never have any chance of happening, because that Friday night, I found myself standing alone beside the snack table. The bass from the music was thumping throughout the whole house, and the waves of chatter made me feel self-conscious for my silence. My back was up against the wall, and I was holding a red plastic cup of lukewarm rum and coke. This party was more unique than I ever could've thought, because it was a party where drag queens strutted down the hall like it was a runway, where girls held each other's hands and where boys were unafraid to slow dance with each other. It made me wonder if Jess had found out about me, but I remembered back to when she handed me the invite; all she had said was, "Here. You seem woke enough." I couldn't find Jess after a while of searching, so there was no hope for her to introduce me to anyone after all. I guess I realized that it would be kind of weird anyway; it would go like, "Hey, glad you could come, there's someone that I think you'd love to meet, especially considering the fact that I know nothing about you." I watched as there were these circles slowly forming, these mini-groups of stereotypes: the guys who wore mascara and nail polish, the chicks who had pixie-cuts and wore at least one thing made of black leather, the group of gamers who could've been trans or bi or gender-fluid. I should've seen it as a beautiful thing that I had stumbled upon—a haven, a place where all these people could come together and be themselves—but it actually made my insides churn to think that I could be lonely even in my own community. The threat of tears jabbed at the backs of my eyes like little pin-needles. I was about to leave then, when someone tapped my shoulder.

She had shoulder-length hair that was smooth and amber like maple syrup, and she had a smile that was warm like a night in July. She looked so friendly, so kind when she smiled. I felt myself tense, and I hoped it wasn't too noticeable. "H-hi," I said, thankful for my casual tone. "Hi," she said, still wearing that sunshine-smile. "Are you here all by yourself?" I nodded, face hotter than a stovetop. I felt those tears coming up again, the familiar burning behind my vision. *She must think I'm pathetic.* "Oh," she said, "well, that's okay. My name's Harlow." She held out her hand, wristbands hanging off her arm like a tangle of rubber vines. I couldn't have asked for a more perfect opportunity to talk to somebody ... but I was afraid. For some reason, fear hit me like a bolt of lightning, and I knew I was afraid because I had a sudden memory: my best friend from sixth grade driving away in his dad's navy 2004 Ford Expedition. I remembered the way that I felt, waving to him by my mailbox with tears coating my cheeks. I was afraid that if I became friends with this person, it would just end up the same way. And I couldn't face that again. So, in front of this sweet stranger, I began to cry like I was a child. Harlow looked alarmed, and she reached out to put her warm hand on my shoulder. "Oh my god, are you okay?" she asked. I just covered my face with my hands and shook my head no. "I-I'm sorry," I managed to sputter out. "I-I'm just panicking and I'm really sad and I'm s-sorry." What was wrong with me? Why couldn't I just stop talking? "You don't have to apologize," Harlow said gently. "If you want to talk about it, I'm here." I did want to tell her everything. I wanted to spill my guts and cry on her shoulder and let her blanket me in her comforting voice and kind words. I felt so stupid, so exposed, and I just couldn't. So, I kind of just walked away, saying, "Sorry to bother you."

Instead of going home, I went to the nearest bathroom and cried because I didn't want people to see me. I kneeled on the tiled floor and let a few sobs escape my throat, immersed in nothing but my shame, embarrassment, loneliness, and the stale aftertaste of sugary alcohol lingering on my tongue. I didn't see why it mattered that I didn't head home. It didn't matter that I was going out the front door with tears spilling and making a mess of my face. I had nothing to hide anyway. I was alone. I had no friends, and no matter how hard I tried, I would never make any. I couldn't achieve something as simple as a handshake and a "nice to meet you." I barely managed hello. There were a million things wrong with me, and in the end, everyone could see it. I prepared myself to sit alone at lunch again with that sinking feeling in the pit of my gut, preventing me from eating anything.

Clara Lick, 11th Grade
Grand Traverse Academy

WARM AND FUZZY
by Joseph Lyons

Kenny walked. He was always walking these days. There was almost never a respite from the movement. The streets were cold; winter had set in over the past few weeks. Its harsh bite was a reminder of years past, when Kenny first lost his home. That first December night was hell: the convulsive shakes and shivers, the slow passage of time, and the uncomfortable realization that he would die cold. The second night had been just as bad. Every night since had been just as bad. The mornings were worse though. He had to walk to stay warm. He would have to stop eventually though, and when he did, the shivering would return. The constant fear of something that he could not stop—the progression of time—haunted his days. That fear was what made the days worse than the nights. At least at night he was too preoccupied with freezing to death to be able to think.

The hard chattering of his teeth was the only sound he could hear other than the cars that raced by and threw slush and mud on the sidewalks. Kenny had quickly learned to sleep in the alleys. Still, those too had dangers. Drunk teenagers would torment anything or anyone they came across. He had to beg for his one threadbare blanket more times than his memory could recall.

Kenny walked into one such alley. The snowfall had been

steady all day, and this crack between buildings was already becoming snow-covered. It was situated between a tobacco store and a closed-down theater. It wasn't a big alley, only ten feet wide, and the ground was hard-packed dirt as opposed to most of the other alleys' cobblestones. The buildings were probably supposed to meet, but last-minute plans when they were built half a century ago must have led to the wasted space. It was also the closest thing Kenny had to a home.

Kenny looked up at the sun; he had traded in his watch for cash a year ago, and could tell it was midafternoon by the location of the sun. Snowflakes fell quickly, sped up by an invisible hand that would whip them back and forth. Ugh. He still had so much walking left to do. Still, today had one upside. His friend Ray was back in town. Ray always took good care of Kenny. He was his only friend since Kenny's wife passed, since he lost his home. Those were painful memories. He had tried a lot of things to cover them up. To an extent they had worked, he could no longer recall what his house had looked like, or how long he had been married. But the pain never left. He could still remember the pain. He could still feel the pain. Kenny looked up again, still midafternoon. Sometimes when he got caught up thinking about his past, hours would fly by without notice. That was always good. He wasn't sure why; before, he had always wanted more time. Now, he just wanted less.

"Hey, Kenny." Ray stood at the end of the alley at the back of the tobacco store. He was smoking something. "Come over here. I got some stuff for you." He smiled warmly. Kenny waved and began walking toward Ray. Kenny had first met him a few months after his wife had died from cancer. The chemo had nearly driven Kenny to bankruptcy. Sarah had tried to call it quits on the radiation multiple times; she would say she didn't want to leave him with nothing when she passed. She had always made more money than Kenny, but he insisted they fight with everything they had.

And when that didn't work, he begged her. He could remember one time in the hospital, he had been on his knees beside her bed, gripping her hand tightly. In the end Sarah's prediction came true. Kenny was left holding her cold hand, begging her to keep fighting.

"Hey Ray, I got money today. Traded in my, uh … I got money today." Ray smiled. The smoke drifting from him smelled sickly sweet.

"Good, how much?" The smirk was still there. Whenever Kenny saw him, Ray always seemed like he was smiling at a joke he had just heard.

"Forty dollars." Ray's smile faded. He quickly glanced down both sides of the alley then back at Kenny.

"That's not enough, man. We've talked about this. Don't schedule a meet-up if you are short-changed. If you need, I know a guy who sells some stuff that's a lot cheaper."

"No, I … uh … I can't do that stuff. It makes me feel everything." Kenny tried to smile, but the worry doomed his attempt to failure. "I just need a bit, Ray. Just something to get through the night. You know I always pay; you know I'm reliable. I can make it up."

Ray shook his head. "That's not good business. You know I can't make a living like that."

"At least you have a living. I gotta get lucky to get this much." Kenny's voice began to rise as the panic began to set in. If he couldn't get the Fentanyl, he would have to face the full brunt of the cold tonight. He'd already gone two days without the relief that the euphoria of the drug provided.

"Calm down, Ken, I always take care of you, don't worry." Ray said, then smiled again as he discarded his joint. "But I need you to help me first."

"I don't have any more money."

"I know, I know. We're past money. But I could use your help moving some of my product." Kenny shook his head no. This was a familiar conversation. Kenny would use the drugs to avoid these horribly cold nights, but he knew his wife would hate him if he tried to profit off his personal damnation. Ray's smile faded again. He had expected Kenny to say yes, this time. "All right you don't have to peddle the stuff. But I can't give you the expensive drugs for nothing." Ray sniffed. "D— it'll be cold tonight. Tell you what: I'll give you some new stuff my supplier just started to crank out. They are still trying to get the ratios right so consider it a free sample." Ray pulled out a small plastic bag from his coat pocket. "It's synthetic, it's supposed to pack a wallop."

"And it'll take the edge off?" Kenny asked.

"It'll make you forget you were bleeding." Ray smiled.

"All right, I need something for tonight. I can't take another night of shaking." Kenny reached out his hand.

"My pleasure." Ray tossed the bag into the alley, then turned and began to walk away. "I'll expect money next time, or you're cut off," Ray said over his shoulder. Kenny's head dropped. He hated when he upset Ray.

"Thanks," Kenny said just above a whisper, then he turned and started to look for the bag. He found it near one wall. It only had two pills inside, one yellow and one red. They were probably the same thing. He opened the bag and took out the yellow pill. He looked at it for a moment. Was this his life? An eternal attempt to forget what he had lost? He tried to swallow the drug. His mouth was gummy, and his saliva was thick. Kenny gagged, trying to swallow. He gagged again and again before he retched the pill back into the snow. D—. Kenny slumped into the alley wall. He hadn't had a drink in two days. His normal public fountain was down for repairs. He needed water though. Kenny reached his hand into the snow bank and grabbed a handful. He then put the snow in his mouth. Pain shot up into his forehead. Once it would have been a sign he was eating his favorite ice cream too fast. But now it heralded the return to a world of quiet things. To a world where he didn't need to walk, or shiver. He could be in peace.

Kenny sat there for a moment, letting the snow melt in his mouth. He needed the water to swallow. His hand was burning. It was strange that cold things could burn you worse than hot. But maybe Kenny had simply forgotten what warm things felt like. The snow melted. His mouth hungrily sucked up the fresh water, absorbing as much as it could. There wasn't much, but it would serve Kenny's purposes. He opened the bag again; he wasn't going to try to find the pill he coughed up. He took out the red pill and swallowed it. It went down easily. Now he just had to wait.

The drug kicked in a lot sooner than the others he had tried. The chill that was always present in the ends of his hands and feet subsided as a heat bled over him. So that was what it felt like. Warmth.

"Hello, friend." Kenny smiled as he lay back into the snow. Another night, hopefully the last.

He woke up the next day shaking harder than ever before. "D—." He had survived again.

Joseph Lyons, 12th Grade
TC West Senior High

UNWELCOME TERRORS
by Joshua Makinson

"Guys... We *really* shouldn't be doing this."

A sheepish looking young boy used his hands to move his lengthy brown hair out of his eyes as he spoke up. He looked ahead to the people he was traveling with--an older boy with black hair, and two girls, both with long blonde hair. The three turned around to look at him, the one boy groaning and falling back to stand next to the complaining kid as the girls waited impatiently.

"Listen, moron. Tonight might be the only chance I get to score with these twins. If you ruin that for me, I'll tell Mom that you caused me trouble, and she'll ground you. Got it?" the older teen threatened his younger brother, aggressively gripping the boy's shoulder.

"Ouch, Phil! I get it! But Mom said—"

"'But Mom specifically said not to leave the house tonight.' I know, I know! When you get older, Jimmy, you get to make some of your own decisions. I'm your older brother, and I decided that tonight we are going out into the woods to have some fun." Phil pushed Jimmy away, Jimmy stumbling as he tried not to fall over from the sudden, abrupt force.

"Stop it! This isn't even fun!" Jimmy said in a loud voice. The two girls, Lora and Abigail, overheard and giggled as they watched the two brothers from a distance. Phil gritted his teeth together in embarrassment as he turned back to his brother.

"You're lucky I even decided to let you come with us. Mom would kill me if she knew I left you at home alone. You're still in seventh grade; you're practically a baby. And since I'm four years older than you, you have to do what I say when I say it. And no more complaining, or I tell Mom that you disobeyed me. Capiche?" Phil's dark blue eyes stared daggers into Jimmy's worried face.

"Fine, whatever," Jimmy said, giving up with a sigh, looking down at his feet and sliding his hands into his pockets.

Phil straightened his leather jacket with a smirk, turning around and walking back to the girls. He went between them and put an arm around both of them, walking deeper into the forest as the girls giggled at his cheesy one-liners.

Jimmy reluctantly followed behind. He kept looking at his feet, kicking a rock along as he followed his brother. He was surprised when they came upon a small, rotting shack in a clearing dimly lit by the moonlight.

"Good, we're here." Phil smiled as he walked up to the shack, sitting down on an overturned log next to the door. The girls sat down next to him, and then Abigail nudged him with her elbow.

"Well, Phil? Did you bring it?" Abigail asked with a casual smile.

"Of course, I did. I always have some on me," Phil bragged as he slipped a small box out of his pocket.

Jimmy was busy examining the shack out of curiosity when he heard a metallic sound. He turned around to see his brother holding a cigarette in his mouth, holding a lighter up to the end as he flicked the flame on. Phil inhaled the smoke, letting it out with a satisfied exhale. Both girls smiled as they reached their hands out. He pulled out two more cigarettes from the box, offering one to each of the girls. They hurriedly took one, and let Phil bring the lighter to their faces to ignite the small tubes.

"Phil! You can't—"

Phil turned around quickly and aggressively. "If you say a word of this to Mom, you're dead." He faced forward again as Abigail and Lora laughed at the younger brother, continuing to enjoy themselves and their smokes.

Jimmy nervously ruffled his own hair. Not only were they too young to smoke, he was sure that Phil had stolen that box of cigarettes from their mother's secret stash that she kept under her bed. No matter what Phil said, they would both be getting a harsh punishment if their mom noticed. He slowly leaned against the old, mossy wall of the cabin, dropping himself to the ground and placing his head between his knees in defeat.

As the smell of tobacco grew stronger, his brother started talking about a time he supposedly beat up a senior. Jimmy, half listening, heard a rustling from beside him. He slowly looked up and froze in terror as something emerged from behind the trees. Out of the foliage came a man wearing a ragged coat. The stranger's hair was brown and covered in dirt as he stumbled into the clearing. The three teens on the log noticed him, and Phil stood up, looking in the intruder's direction.

"Who are you?" Phil asked in a menacing manner. The man groaned in response, drawing closer.

"I said, who ARE you?" He pushed the man, who fell backward, the girls gasping as the weird person fell without any resistance.

Jimmy's face turned pale. The man got back up but supported himself on all fours. He crab-walked slowly toward his attacker, his head dangling downward between his shoulders.

"W-what? Stay away!" Phil yelled as he threw his cigarette at the man. The stranger screeched, lunging into him and digging his nails into Phil's throat. Jimmy choked on his own breath, standing up as he helplessly watched the man bend down and bite into his brother's throat with a meaty crunch.

The blonde girls screamed in terror, dropping their lit smokes as the man turned his attention to them. Both of them began to shout even louder, holding onto each other for dear life. The bloody crawler jumped forward onto the log, pinning both girls down with his hands. He pushed hard as his hands completely fell into their stomachs, ceasing their ear-piercing screams of horror.

Jimmy felt his pants become warm and wet as he saw the man pull handfuls of slippery entrails out from the bodies of the Lora and Abigail, shoveling them into his mouth like a starving lion. Jimmy began to step backward when he tripped over a branch, causing him to fall onto his back with an exclamation of pain. The murderous creature turned around to the source of the sound, making Jimmy's face turn completely white with fear.

The being slowly crawled toward Jimmy, and he just sat there, eyes wide and filled with tears. He clasped his hands over his mouth as the creature drew closer. It stood over him, jaw drooling with blood. It seeped onto Jimmy's face, dripping rapidly from his forehead to the edge of his hands that he kept suctioned to his mouth. Jimmy cried intensely as he tried to prevent himself from screaming.

The man's head was turned oddly. He had dark red slits where his eyes should have been, and his skin was gray and leathery. His hair looked like scorched seaweed covered in mud. Jimmy noticed no nose or nostrils on the face and fixed his gaze only on the bloody teeth in the hungry creature's mouth. It brought its face close to his, and Jimmy squeezed his eyes shut in preparation for his final breath. He waited in fear as the creature breathed heavily into his face, the smell of flesh and guts heavy on its tongue. To his surprise, the creature backed up after another minute, slowly returning to the body of Phil, reaching its crimson-stained hands back into the hole torn into the older brother's neck.

Jimmy's stomach rose and fell with intensity as he threw up in his mouth. Not risking letting it out and making more noise, he clenched his eyes shut once more and swallowed the rank brew with tears of agony. He slowly stood up again, the sound of his feet masked by the gluttonous slurps of the monster standing over his brother's corpse. Slowly, Jimmy backed away from the scene, turning around and sprinting as fast as he could once the shack became hidden behind the dark trees.

He knew they shouldn't have gone out there.

Joshua Makinson, 12th Grade
Kalkaska High School

DRAGON HEART
by Jesse L Martin

Up on a mountain top, high above the clouds, where the enormous peaks of stone are powdered in the cold, heavy snow, there lies a cave, lit ever so carefully by the flame of the unconquerable beast. The lair not layered with gold, nor with metal or bones. Not full of the smell of sulfur nor bodies of lost adventurers that wandered a little too close. Not any of these awfully crude, smelly things. None at all. Rather, this is the lair of a creature who cares not for violence or blood, but more for the finer things in life. There is a wine cellar with the most peculiar flavors within the wooden framework made of a dark Boreal Oak, crafted by only the finest of dwarven carpenters. On the same floor, there is a cheese room, with wheels big enough to feed a village for months. A layer down, in the most humid part of the luxurious cave, dwell his cigars, kept in peak condition, as the massive chamber acts as a humidor. Although it is said he doesn't keep gold layered upon the floor of his cave, he has halls upon halls with glass casings housing the finest of jewels: rubies, sapphire, amber, and jade. In the foyer, massive quartz crystals jut out from the floors, carved into a fountain of a divine presence.

A stranger knocks at the massive Boreal door. The gentle thud of a large creature can be heard from the door. The lithe figure clad in rags backs away in anticipation of the coming. A hollow, low creak emits from the brass hinges and the door swings open to the face of a dark red dragon, smiling warmly down at the visitor.

"What brings you to my humble abode, little one?" he bellows.

The young stranger looks up from beneath her cowl revealing the delicate features of a young female face and smiles brightly as she stretches her arms out.

"I was on a quest to hug a dragon," she says.

The great beast releases a hearty laugh and crouches down to be within the small child's reach.

"You came to the right dragon, my child," he says as he stretches his fragile arms out to embrace the small child.

They come together and the child can feel the safe warmth of the dragon's chest pressing against hers, the breathing and the heartbeat. They feel as though they are one. They part and the great beast looks down at her.

"Where do you live, my child? I can get someone to fly you home," he asks warmly.

She slowly gazes down and begins to cry. The Dragon embraces her with another long, caring hug, wrapping her up in his withered wings, shielding her from the unforgiving cold.

"Do not cry, my child, join me by the fire and tell me your story," he says, beckoning her to the warmth and safety of the hearth. "Here your stomach and heart will be full, and your mind at peace," he says with a sparkle in his eye, hiding the sadness beneath.

The immense dragon moves away from the doorway and waves his aged claw, inviting the young stranger in. The child takes a deep breath, wipes the tears from her eyes and walks into the massive chamber, the deep red carpet concealing the cold stone beneath, accents of gold placed among the massive dark wood furnishings. A roaring fire resides within the hearth, the crackling of pine and oak bounces about the room, mixing with the trickling of the quartz fountain. On the mantle, there lie amulets of jade, jewels adorned with gold plating and smooth granite stones, perfectly spherical. In front of the fire, there is a single chair, red velvet cushions placed delicately upon the masterful carpentry. The dragon gestures to the chair and the girl wipes the tears from her eyes and finds her way to the seat. As she sits down the dragon lies down upon the floor, his tail stretching from one end of the room to the other, curling around the perimeter.

"Now," he says in a soft tone, "What is your story, little one?"

Jesse L. Martin, 11th Grade
Traverse City Central High School

THE PLACE WHERE GOOD MEN GO
by Caleb Mitchell-Ward

Prrrrop. They had an assault rifle on the roof and the mud wall we crouched behind was covered in machine-gun holes. The firing stopped, and Mohamed and I could hear the man softly cursing. I nodded to Mohamed and we kicked back the rubble blocking the door, then with only one other officer we surrounded the man on the roof.

"Open your shawl!!" I yelled.

He was clear of bombs. I zip-tied his hands then handed him to Yafiz.

"Mohamed," I said waving to him.

We hopped off the roof into a dusty garden and started to search the house. A man came rushing out with his Kalashnikov. I shot him twice in the chest with my pistol before he could raise his gun and he fell to the ground. The last rooms were clear, so we grabbed the body and left. Yafiz was waiting by the door with the prisoner and we dropped the body to talk with him.

"Are we going to pull the flag down?" asked Yafiz.

It was a piece of black cloth loosely attached to a long stick and it moved gently from the wind.

"No, let's leave it up. That way his friends will think it's still safe for them and they'll come in shooting range."

Mohamed and I threw the body of the dead fighter in a ditch because it was too hot to bury him midday and as he hit the dry ditch bottom the folds of his white hijab, bloodstained and powdered with dust, fell back from his face. He was a man younger than me, probably a teenager, with a hopeful face and piercing blue eyes.

"Let's go," said Mohamed, slapping me on the shoulder as he walked to the Humvee. Yafiz put the prisoner in the backseat with me and Mohamed before starting to drive back toward town. The Humvee, you could say, was a gift from America. I remember when the Americans came into our town for the first time, their wide-brimmed tanks caking the houses behind them in dust from the road, the town greeting their arrival. But now they were gone. The only ones who came into our town now were Dostum's men; the Taliban stayed only in the outskirts, sometimes getting left behind in their retreat from the police, like the fighter sitting across from me now. He had a narrow face, a deep black beard, and cold eyes, which looked calmly ahead. They always looked so calm. I could tell it was making Mohamed uneasy by the way he eyed the man and kept his finger hovering over the trigger of his Kalashnikov, steady even as the Humvee went across bumps in the road. I looked out the scratched window, yellow from the sun, onto the dust of a dead wheat field with tassels of sand spinning across it. The trees of town appeared in the window, tall against the wide stretch of dead earth rising into the bare mountain slopes that were crowned with the pure white snows of Hindu Kush, distant and hazy in the hot air. Driving through the narrow street, lined by crammed mud and rock houses, we passed a child leading a goat on a rope to market. We parked by the police station, which was on top of the rise in town, right by the mosque. The station was built from mud and stone, like everything else in Abdan. Abdullah Mazari, the police chief, was sitting at a table when we arrived; the light that streamed through a hole in the wall shone onto his thin black mustache and a childlike face.

"You got one!"

He looked happy.

"Aryo, that's my boy. Did he give you much trouble?"

"There were some machine gun rounds fired but nothing we couldn't handle."

"That's good, that's good. Listen, you and Mohamed do your nightly sweep, then I think you should be done for the day."

I thanked him and then Mohamed and I left and walked across town before going to the outskirts because nothing ever happened in town. In a field on the side of the main road, the elders were playing *Buzkashi*. So we watched for a while as they reared and whipped their horses, whose muscles moved beneath their tight brown skin and hooves dragged and hit the ground, making the dust rise and turn gold from the dusk sun so that the men and the horses became only shadows that shifted in one mass of struggle. It was almost dark when we left.

The sky was pink above the black mountains. We sat at a wood table beneath the glow of a lantern outside the inn, watching the mountains and drinking tea.

I couldn't sleep that night and I often couldn't sleep, not because of the heat of the summer night, but because of the distant booms and piercing whistles of mortar shells being shot off by the Taliban in the towns around us, or sometimes right by the city edges, sometimes all night. So, I lay in my cot, staring at the ceiling. There was a sweet smell in the room. I turned and saw Rashid, who lay in the bed next to me smoking opium from a long pipe.

"Do you want any?"

I shook my head.

"You sure? It'll help you sleep."

"No, I'm fine."

Mohamed walked down the stairs that went to the roof.

"Hey, you should come and see the fireworks show."

"Sure, I'm not going to sleep anyway."

From the roof of the barracks I could see over the town and the country beyond it, where the mortars, sometimes illuminating the trees and soldiers around them as they were fired, made blazing orange arcs that cut across the sky and burst into flame with faint thuds when they landed and were followed by the gold spray of bullets.

"So, you couldn't sleep?"

"No."

"Why."

"Because of that kid I shot."

Another mortar shell cracked far away.

"I know, you know, that kids grow up quick here."

"Too quick."

"You probably killed a man."

"I've killed too many men already. I'm getting sick of it."

"That's why you're a good man."

"I keep thinking that this isn't a place for good men."

"The only place for good men is heaven, my friend."

"We're on our way there fast."

"On that happy thought, I think I'm going to go to bed."

"Ok."

"Goodnight."

"Goodnight."

The shells kept booming all night, but I finally slept. Then early in the morning, I woke up to the banging of metal on metal.

"Wake up, men, we have an emergency," said Abdullah.

It was still dark, but early enough that my mother would be

awake. I used to live with her in the house at the edge of town, and we had livestock and a wheat field, and she still farmed even though she didn't keep the livestock. I knocked on the door.

"Who is it? Who is ..."? She opened the door.

"It's me, Ma."

"Oh, come in. Tea?"

"No, thank you."

We sat together in the eating room.

"So, what made you stop by?"

"I... I'm going on a trip, uh ... for the police, and I wanted to say goodbye to you before I went."

"Really... Uh... Uh... Well... Uh...when are you going to be back, are you going to be gone for long?"

"I don't know, Ma. That's why I wanted to come and see you."

"You be safe on this trip. Ok?"

"Ok."

"Ok."

There was a knock on the door. It was Mohamed.

"It's almost dawn, so I thought I should come get you."

"Yeah, I'm coming."

"Goodbye, Ma, I have to go."

"Ok, son. I'll see you later."

"Yes, Ma. Goodbye."

It was almost light outside and the eastern clouds were orange. I walked with Mohamed to the barracks, where I dressed in the combat gear that we got from the Americans, a bulletproof vest and helmet and a strap for my Kalashnikov cartridges with two filled canteens strapped beneath it. I grabbed my Kalashnikov and pistol then walked to the front of the station. The first Humvee pulled up to us with the two Humvees from Kholm behind it. Yafiz crouched over with his helmet off, vomiting. We all got into the first Humvee. I could see town from my window and the clouds flashing with white light as they gathered against the mountains, and the long dark lines of rain falling from the clouds onto the empty fields. We passed the remnants of a Russian tank, and it made me think of all the places I'd been in the past, more places than most of the people in Abdan. While on a tour with the police force, years ago, when NATO was still here I had seen the white doves perch on the sea-blue domes of Mazar-i-Sharif and the old mud houses of Tashkurgan spread beneath the long gray ridges where the cold wind blew down from Bam-i-Dunya.

Gajan came into view in the front windshield an hour after we left. Black smoke rose from behind the yellow stone walls and a woman in a *burqa* and her kid, who had sandy hair and wide eyes, walked past the Humvee. The poplar grove was feet in front of us, but the Humvee stopped.

"There's an IED," said Yafiz.

Rashid hopped out from the passenger seat with the stick he was going to use to remove it. Then after a moment, I heard the thud of a bullet from outside. The driver talked in a panicked way to Abdullah from his radio. I stood up so I could see out of the front windshield. Rashid was rolled over on his back with blood spreading from his head onto the black road, and the woman and her kid were running into a field. They must have had a sniper on the city wall.

"Abdullah says go!" yelled the driver.

"Did you tell him what just happened?" I asked.

"He said go. GO now!"

I opened the door and Mohamed and Yafiz and I ran to the edge of the road, hiding behind the trees. A poppy field went all the way to the city wall and along it was a dry irrigation canal. I slid into the canal and kept low, so my head was hidden below the poppy bulbs. They moved side to side in the wind and some had cuts on them and dried liquid from the opium harvest. Even in the shade of the poppies, it was very hot, so we stopped and drank from our canteens. We stared at the ground, drinking in silence because there was nothing to talk about, other than the fact that we might die. I didn't want to die because I knew the feeling of drinking cold water in the heat and tea in the evening, and that was enough to make me want to live. A spurt of bullets hit something far away, probably the Humvees.

"Those jerks. They're not going to get shot," said Mohamed.

"Ha." Yafiz smiled.

We sat drinking for a while longer.

"All right, let's go, we're almost to the city," I said.

The canal kept going and ran alongside the stone wall then ended at a small gravel road heading to the city. We crawled to the edge of the road. The road ended at a green door and above it, on the wall, a Taliban fighter paced nervously with his Kalashnikov.

"Mohamed, can you get him?" I asked.

"Yeah, but when I do, you and Yafiz have to run to the door."

Mohamed eyed his shot carefully and fired and the man fell back off the wall.

"GO!"

Once we came to the wall, bullets burst from the other side and tore up the door, sending pieces of wood through the air. I waited until the firing stopped and counted to three on my hand. I pushed the door open and Yafiz and Mohamed rushed in behind me. A gunman stood in front of us, confused, and Yafiz shot him and then a man came down a tower by the wall. I shot him in the head. Deeper in the city two fighters walking side by side saw us and the road exploded in crackling gunfire. I grabbed Yafiz by the collar and pulled him into the room at the bottom of the tower. Dust rose from the small craters made by bullets as they hit the ground in front of us. Mohamed ran into the tower and rested his Kalashnikov on its handle while grabbing the rifle butt and put one finger on the trigger so that he could shoot them without being hit. Something hit the ground near us that wasn't a bullet, so Mohamed looked past the doorway. After a second he stood up and walked out of my view. The room crackled loudly with gunshots again. I ran to save Mohamed but he was standing calmly in front of two dead Taliban, one lying in the middle of the road and the other leaned against a doorway.

"We should go," I said to him.

"Yeah."

We knew that when we came into the city, we had made too much noise to go on unnoticed, so it was best for us to hide. We ran up the staircase in the tower. There was a door at the top that opened to a walkway going along the wall, where we could see the stacked and sun-stained mud houses that cast shadows on the narrow alleys and smaller buildings of the city. There was another tower diagonal to us, which I pointed at and everyone else nodded. We ran to it, crouched and threw the door open then closed it. No one fired at us. We went down a stairway in the tower that led into a dusty square, empty except for a rubble pile on the far wall that had an open doorway next to it. I led Mohamed and Yafiz to the doorway cautiously. POW! Blood sprayed from Yafiz's head and he fell back in the doorway where he had stood. Mohamed rushed in front of Yafiz's body with his finger held down on the trigger. I could hear the sound of boots stomping on the ground from across the other wall. There was only one way out now. I ran up the rubble pile.

"Mohamed!!" I couldn't reach the top of the wall. As he ran toward me I shot the fighters coming through the doorway and dropped the rifle when he was next to me, then helped him onto the wall, and he pulled me up over its edge. There was a platform in front of us that we crawled toward as bullets burst the mud of the low, cracked ridge between us and the square. Mohamed slammed open a trapdoor at the top of the platform and dropped down, landing on his back in the room below. I closed it as I dropped and landed next to him on a cool sandy floor. There were no doors or openings in the room, except for the one we fell in through and a small square hole we couldn't reach. We leaned against the wall and drank from our canteens.

"What the hell are we going to do, Aryo?"

"I don't know. Try the radio."

He unhitched it from his rifle strap and spun the top dial until he was on the right wavelength.

"This is recon team, we need cover for a retreat. Located roughly 30 feet south of the west entrance. Is cover possible? Over."

Prrrrrr. The radio crackled from static and gunshots.

"Request for cover is not possible. Frontal assault is delayed. Over."

"F—!!" Mohamed threw the radio and it broke against the wall.

"How many bullets do you have?" he asked.

"Not many."

He sighed and I sighed.

"So, this is it then. This is where we die."

"Yeah, maybe so."

"You know I didn't even get to say goodbye to my mother."

Mohamed was almost crying.

"I didn't know you had one."

"Yeah, she's a little ways out of Abdan."

We were both staring at the wall.

"It's a shame about Yafiz. He was still just a kid."

"Yeah."

Mohamed looked like he was going to say something but stopped.

"You don't seem that afraid," he said.

"No, I'm scared too. I've just learned not to cry over my fate."

"So, you're ready then?"

"For what?"

"To go to the place where good men go."

"When you put it that way, maybe so."

"I know you'll be there."

"No, I've done some terrible things."

"So has everyone."

The sounds of gunfire and stamping feet were close to us now.

"Il a al-iqqa my brother."

"Il a al-iqqa."

I knew that even though I would be dead soon, the towns would still ring with prayer in the morning and a Taliban leader would spray bullets into the air in celebration of last night's slaughter. And the wind, always the wind, would sweep down cold across the land.

Caleb Mitchell-Ward, 11th Grade
Central High School

DEVIL'S PLAY
by Zoe Moseler

The ruins cast shadows
along the deserted hills,
with a scythe-shaped moon
reaching down upon
its victims.

No laughter or voices are
heard at this place for its residents
have long since disappeared.

On the cliff's edge, you can
hear the ocean waves crashing,
the skeletons of countless
victims float upon its
foamy broth.

An orange glow is cast
upon the forgotten
land as a single flame
flickers. It never burns out

nor will it ever for it signifies
the fallen, the damned, and
the murderous.

This place is the devil's,
his personal entertainment.
Demons dance upon the falling
stone of castles long ago and
for one night a year, they may
leave this sacred place

to add residence to the flaming
gates and symphony of screams that
occur when the doors are left open.

Zoe Moseler, 12th Grade
Suttons Bay

AMERICA'S WEAKNESS
By Zoe Moseler

It's been around for millennia
like the constant wind blowing
Whether it was the great looming
Columns of Rome
or the quiet rice fields of China
it's wrought havoc upon empires
Women are not delicate like lilies
that must be protected
They are tempests awaiting
a ship
not a man
One person is not enough
It could take more than an army
marching upon the gates of hell
Not a single Malala
nor a Ruth Bader Ginsburg
could change the tides
With a glass ceiling
as high as
the Empire State Building
it feeling impossible to reach
If a fire were started
Like that of the great Peshtigo Fire
the Syskiyou Fire
or the Chapleau-Mississagi Fire
then maybe the sweet call
of equality could be heard
So many voices all at once
like a pack of wolves
or a unified meditation chant

or the wail of police sirens
Why does our country sit by
Like a Cardinal in prayer
as acts of assault occur
Assaults like Nassar's
or Weinstein's
or Trump's
Land of the intolerant
and home of
the disillusioned

Zoe Moseler, 12th Grade
Suttons Bay

AN EPISTLE TO LOVE
by Reann Nelson

Ever since I was a little girl
I had heard of you
And wanted to meet you.

You were a friend
Of my parents
My sister and her
Husband.

I never understood
why my friends
ran and screamed,
'Cooties.'

I was excited
When you introduced me
To him.

That makes
You and me
friends now.

But
why is
my body
searing?

Why did I turn around
and see that
he
was gone?

But you
were there,
knife coated
in crimson
from its sheath
in my back.

Where you plunged it.

And here I thought,
You were my friend.

I, TOO, SING AMERICA

After Walt Whitman and Langston Hughes

by Reann Nelson

I, too, sing America.

I am the youthful wind of change sweeping over the nation.
It pressures me to succeed so I may accomplish what the ones before me could not,
Spending late nights knee-deep in studies,
Drowning in my own inhibitions,
And wishing there were someone who understood.

Tomorrow,
I'll be off to college.
Society will regret making me work so hard,
And making me grow up so fast,
Just now realizing all the little things I missed.
I'll make my life my own, finally free.
Promising myself I'll do better when I have children,
Only to fall into the neat box that was set out for me from the
        beginning.

Besides,
Our nation will look at my life and feel ashamed—
Seeing that it has condemned me and those after me to the same
        suffering.

I, too, sing America.

Reann Nelson, 11th Grade
Glen Lake Community Schools

SIX HUNDRED AND ONE SECONDS
by Riley Kate Robinson

CAST OF CHARACTERS

ALLYSON FORD — Twenty-two. English major. Sweater lover and poet. Often drinks chocolate milk for breakfast. Has a very large stack of books to read yet can't stop buying more.

JESSE PORTER — Twenty-three. Always smiling. Premature teller of dad jokes. Has to get out of bed on the *literal* right side every day. Smells of rose and sandalwood.

JIM CARSON — Age unknown. Announces speed-dating at the bar on Friday nights and bingo at the senior center on Sunday afternoons. Wears sweater vests. Sweats more than the average human being.

Scene
Max's Taphouse in Baltimore, Maryland.
A wintry street in downtown Baltimore.

Time
The present.

Scene One

AT RISE: A noisy bar in Baltimore, Maryland.

A soundtrack of incoherent chatter plays in the background.

ALLYSON is sitting alone at a two-person table parallel to the audience with her head resting in her hand.

A bell rings over top of the chatter. JESSE walks on stage from the left. He approaches ALLYSON's table and places a hand on the back of the empty chair across from her.

JIM CARSON is standing behind a microphone in the corner of the room.

JIM
THIS IS IT, LADIES AND GENTS, THE LAST MATCH OF THE NIGHT! Get your cards out and make sure to get their ticket number... and their phone number of course, in case you want a round two! Your last ten minutes of the night beginnnn... NOW!

JESSE
So, I guess this is me? I'm Jesse.

(ALLYSON smiles as JESSE sits down. She holds out her hand and he shake it. JIM CARSON steps up to the microphone.)

ALLYSON
Allyson. What brings you here tonight? We have what? Ten minutes? That's a short amount of time, don't you think? Ten minutes to find out everything about a complete stranger.

JESSE
We aren't complete strangers; first name basis is the foundation of a new relation——friendship. You know, whatever you're looking for. I'm kind of new to the speed dating scene. My roommate, Corey, dragged me here. He's over there.

(Points his finger over his shoulder stage right.)

And if the first name thing doesn't convince you, I'm twenty-three, a hard-core fan of 80s hair bands, and I love watching Jeopardy. See? Now you know me.

ALLYSON

All right then, Scorpions or Bon Jovi?

JESSE

C'mon, that's easy! Scorpions all the way! "No One Like You," "Still Loving You," "Big City Nights," "Rock You Like a Hurricane"? Those are masterpieces.

ALLYSON

Who doesn't pick Bon Jovi? What about "Bed of Roses"? Or "Wanted Dead or Alive"? Have you ever even seen *Deadliest Catch*? My dad would totally be shaking his head right now.

(Both chuckle.)

JESSE

They're not too bad, I guess. What's your favorite type of ice cream? Choose wisely and I *might* be able to forgive you for your last answer.

ALLYSON

Hear me out on this one, its vanill—

JESSE (Raising his voice dramatically.)

VANILLA?

ALLYSON

I said hold on! Its vanilla with chocolate sauce mixed into it. It's the perfect chocolate ice cream, not too boring but not too chocolatey. Now *that's* a true masterpiece. You'll have to try it sometime. Absolutely heaven. I'm guessing you're more of a mint chocolate chip?

JESSE

Butter pecan, actually.

ALLYSON
Huh, you and my great-aunt Gladys would get along nicely.

JESSE
She sounds remarkable.

ALLYSON
I'm just pulling your leg, I don't actually have a great-aunt Gladys. However, that does sound eighty-year-old womanish.

JESSE
I'll wear that title, I have no shame. Hey, if we are going to be friends, I just thought I would tell you right off the bat: I have kleptomania. But don't worry, when it gets really bad, I take something for it.
    (ALLYSON's face lights up and she smiles as she lets out a hearty laugh.)

ALLYSON
That was probably one of the cheesiest things I have ever heard.

JESSE
I like to practice my standup comedy, whenever I can. I was a little nervous to crack it out tonight though, after all we are sitting down.

ALLYSON
Oh my gosh. Ha ha ha, what a punny guy.

JESSE
Obviously I have quite a bit of work to do. Cheesy jokes are kinda my thing; instead of *People Magazine*, I use joke books as my bathroom reading.

ALLYSON
That's awesome. I read, but definitely not those kinds of books. I'll have to look into them more. Maybe we can have a "joke-off" sometime.

JESSE

For sure, I'm always willing to outwit an unsuspecting victim. I would throw in a construction joke, buuut I'm still working on them. And I can't give away all my best materials out on the first erm, *date*.

ALLYSON

Now *that's* what I'm talking about! Anything else you want to know?

JESSE

Favorite Christmas movie?

ALLYSON

Easy, *Elf.* If you could go to any place in the world where would you go?

JESSE

Real? Greece. Fictional—

BOTH

Hogwarts! Wait seriously? No way! Twins!

JESSE

Ravenclaw?

ALLYSON

Holy cow! I guess we have more in common than we thought!

JESSE

Yeah, maybe you aren't too bad after all.

    (Both smile.)

However, you actually never answered why you are here in the first place.

ALLYSON

Would you believe me if I told you that it was my grandma who convinced me to come? She goes to bingo every Sunday and I guess this guy is the caller. He must have told the seniors about it because one day she is bugging me about "not putting myself out there enough" and the next thing I know she is telling me she signed me up for this gig. It's not too bad actually. The first guy was a little creepy. During the whole ten minutes he probably blinked six times. Then the second guy must have not realized that there would be appetizers at this thing because his breath smelled like he had eaten multiple tuna sandwiches before coming. We are at a bar for Pete's sake!

JESSE

Dang, your grandma is really looking out for ya, huh? Everyone should have someone like her to get the ball rolling. So, what about guys three through six? Got any leads?

ALLYSON

Eh, each one is just as "interesting" as the last, I guess. Jury's still out on #6 though. I still have a few more questions, the answers to which could make or break it. Favorite pizza topping?

JESSE

Mushrooms and spinach, and seriously Al, if the next word that comes out of your mouth has anything to do with pine and apple, I'm walking out.

ALLYSON

Don't worry, I would never. That goes against my own personal ten commandments. However, I am slightly judging your decisions as well. Mushroom, eh, I could live with, but spinach? It just gets shriveled and I just don't really vibe with that. I'm more of a traditional pepperoni gal. Why change what has always worked? Honestly, you know what? Let's leave, like right now. Why not? We have nothing to lose. Let's go get pizza or tuna sandwiches? We've already gotten to know each other so the breath can't be too off-putting anymore. Besides, we would just be sitting here for five more minutes. There are much better things we could be doing.

JESSE

What about Corey? He was kind of my ride and I don't know if I could just leave him, how would I get home?

ALLYSON

I can drive you home, and I think Corey will be fine. He seems pretty preoccupied with the chick with the pink hair anyway. Plus, what am I going to do, kidnap you? I told you my Hogwarts house, and that is something I only share with my closest of friends. C'mon #6, the world awaits.

(End Scene.)

Scene Two

> AT RISE: JESSE and ALLYSON can be seen walking down a snowy street downtown. The windows are decorated for Christmas and snowflakes are gently falling around them.

JESSE

Did you see their faces when we walked out? Some of them looked like they needed to be rescued from the antichrist.
 (JESSE sighs and runs a hand through his hair.)

In how many circumstances do you think speed dating actually works out? I mean, like you said before, you are only given ten minutes to learn years' worth of information.

ALLYSON

I'm not sure, but think about all the people that audition for shows like *The Bachelor*, are those marriages real? The guy dates like thirty women for a couple of months and then is supposed to confess his true love to one of them? It must take a special person to put themselves in either position.

JESSE

Actually, it's more like 25 women, but uh...I don't watch it so I mean I don't know.

(ALLYSON laughs.)

Do you believe in love at first sight? Like real, true love?

ALLYSON

I'm not really sure about that either, is it love at first sight? Or lust? I honestly don't know. I definitely believe in interest at first sight and love over time. But right away? If it was love at first sight, then I think the proposal comes at about the six-and-a-half-minute mark according to speed dating etiquette. What about fate? Do you believe in that?

(JESSE is quiet for a moment.)

JESSE

Yeah, I think I do. Maybe just not in like this whole "your life has been planned out from the moment you were born" type of thing." I just don't know how else to explain those feelings where you can't really explain why you need to go somewhere or do something other than the fact that you just need to. Like what are the odds your grandma signed you up for the same night my bird-brained roommate dragged me along, and that we just so happened to be sitting exactly in the position that we would meet for the last ten minutes. I mean we have quite literally known each other for all of five minutes, and it's not like I am confessing my love for you just yet, I'm not one to jump the gun, but I just feel as though we were meant to sit across from each other for ten minutes. I quite literally feel as though I could tell you anything, and you wouldn't judge me for a second. Well, minus the whole butter pecan situation but I can get over that one.

ALLYSON

No, I totally get that and I agree, I doubt that all of this was by pure accident. Truth be told, at first, I just went because I wanted to make my grandmother happy but yet, I also had a feeling that something extraordinary would come out of this. I mean, if it weren't for you, I could be stuck getting cornered by Tuna Breath. Yet here we are. If everything were pre-planned maybe we still would have left early, except with different people and we would be glued to lord knows who behind a bush, or in an alley. But we aren't, you know? Who knows what will happen a week from now, or a month, or six months. All I'm saying is that I'm perfectly fine with this. I don't want ten minutes to learn *everything* about someone, that's not enough. I would certainly hope that most people are more complex than to be able to explain and express themselves in just ten minutes.

JESSE

That's a very good point, but what if everyone just had a ten-minute story? Think about us. *We* have a ten-minute story. Not even. Seven minutes and counting.

ALLYSON

Who says our story is only ten minutes?

JESSE

The sweaty guy up on the stage at the bar.

ALLYSON

Well, he's wrong. We have plenty of time. A whole lifetime of time. We just can't waste it. People waste too much time doing things so unimportant in the grand scheme of things. But enough of the deep scary stuff, back to the essentials. What's your favorite color?

JESSE

Purple. Favorite food?

ALLYSON

Macaroni. Favorite season?

JESSE

Winter, there is something about the snowfall that just makes me feel so in love with the world.

(ALLYSON and JESSE continue to walk along the side walk in silence. After a little while JESSE slips his hand into ALLYSON's.)

JESSE
Dogs or cats?

ALLYSON
It's a very close race, but I think cats are a whisker ahead. What about you?

JESSE
I don't think I could pick, but my red lab, Bella, at home would definitely tell me to lean toward the former.

ALLYSON
Well, I guess I will have to meet her then to see what she has against cats.

JESSE
That would be quite the conversation.

(ALLYSON continues to walk but JESSE comes to a standstill.)

JESSE
Hold up a minute.

(Tugging on her hand, JESSE pulls ALLYSON back and softly places a kiss on her lips.)

ALLYSON
You know what? I think this is exactly where I was supposed to be tonight. Here, with you, and the snow, and just everything. It was meant to be exactly like this and something out there in the universe knew it too. Action movies or comedy?

JESSE
Both, but like not separately. The action movie has to be funny. I'm

a deep philosophical guy when I need to be, but I mean c'mon, if a superhero isn't cracking jokes while he's kicking some villain's butt then what's the point? Ketchup or ranch?

    (ALLYSON bursts out laughing)

ALLYSON
Depends on what I'm eating it with. Chicken? Ketchup. Pizza? Ranch. How do you see yourself in ten years? That kinda just jumped off of the deep end but, if this is our first date, I need to know what to expect. Ya know?

JESSE
I usually just do what I feel is right in the moment. However, I've been thinking about it and really? I'm going to school for accounting so hopefully working at my own firm, and I want to get married. But I don't want just your typical white picket fence. I want something more out there. Maybe a yellow fence or blue. We would have three or four kids with their toys strewn in the backyard. And a large dining room where we can have big dinners on Sunday afternoons with both of our families. Something more than average. Something astonishing. Have you ever thought about it?

ALLYSON
I mean yeah, every girl has. But to be completely honest that sounds wonderful.

JESSE
It's Jesse Porter by the way. I forgot to say that earlier. They should really give us nametags instead of these stupid huge numbers.

    (JESSE pulls off this large sticker with the number 16 on it.)

ALLYSON
Ford, but not associated with the cars or anything, it's just our small Midwestern family. I'm from Minnesota but I moved out here from school. I'll probably stay out here. A yellow and blue fence is sounding pretty good right about now.

JESSE
If you were given three wishes, what would you wish for?

ALLYSON
First, I would wish to be able to speak every language possible, that way I could travel anywhere and still be able to speak to everyone without barriers. Secondly, I would wish for everyone to love and accept each other completely unselfishly. And finally, I would honestly save my third wish for later. Everything else is exactly the way I want it.

(The snow picks up and the wind gets stronger.)

We should probably head back to our cars, it's getting pretty unruly out here.

(They walk back until they get to the end of the street.)

JESSE
You know what, maybe I don't believe in love at first sight, but I do believe in love at the 601st second.

ALLYSON
Why 601?

JESSE
Because that is officially ten minutes and one second. The exact time our story becomes our own.

(JIM CARSON's voice sounds through the auditorium, he is not seen onstage.)

JIM
Well, I always knew these Friday night shindigs would work out for somebody. Crazy kids.

END PLAY

Riley Kate Robinson, 11th Grade
Bellaire

HEAD OVER HEELS
by Emma Ryan

Once soft and loving, the Prince's hands were now tainted with the blood of his comrades—the blood of his army, the blood of his friends. The hilt of Achilles' sword was heavy in Conan's calloused palm; he was not a swordsman, but it was the first weapon he could grab as the ambush began. The strong copper smell of blood lingered heavily in the air, and crimson pursed up around the leather of his boots as he walked through the swamp of bodies that surrounded him. Blood was everywhere, and he was unaware of what was his and what was the blood of his army men. Silence rang in his ear; the silence of death is deafening. Prince Conan, the furthest thing from a skilled swordsman, and Achilles, the leader of the revolution fighting hand in hand to slaughter a whole legion of army men—Conan's army men. Conan knew that any survivors would carry word of betrayal to the King. The sound of choked, angry sobs broke the silence. Conan turned to find his lover plunging a broken arrow into the chest of a fallen soldier over and over again. There was an anger in his eyes, an anger that Conan had never seen before.

"Achilles..." Conan spoke softly, placing a gentle hand on his shoulder. "He's dead, they're all dead, you can stop now—" Achilles' arm swung around, and Conan froze as he felt the sting of the blade against his cheek and the warmth of his blood trickling down his jaw. The prince felt his eyes swell with tears, blurring his vision and threatening to spill as he took a step away from Achilles. He watched as his eyes changed from a murderous sneer, to a gentle gaze full of regret.

"Conan, I'm sorry, I really am, I-I didn't mean to—" Achilles stuttered, climbing to his feet and extending his arms to pull him close in a loving embrace, but Conan took another step back.

"... Conan?" Achilles begged again. Conan looked down at the body at his feet, then back at Achilles as tears spilled over his eyelids and fell down his cheeks like a waterfall. The prince dashed off into the forest, pushing through shrubs and broken branches, running so fast that he could hardly keep a hold of his footing.

Conan never cried, or at least not since he was nineteen when his mother passed away. Now here he was, blinded by hot tears that streamed down his face as he tripped over shrubs and fallen trees. Low branches whipped his face, but the stinging pain could not compare to the fire in his lungs and the copper taste in the back of his throat that seemed to rip open at the scent of fresh air. It all happened so fast, he was dizzy at the memory.

Conan wrapped his arms around a tree. His mouth felt like cotton and his legs wanted to break out from underneath him, but the only thing on his mind was "Run. Get far away. Go back to the kingdom. Now you know why Achilles is the leader of this revolution—he's a ruthless killer, just like Father told you." He pressed his forehead against the rough bark of the tree, dry heaving on nothing but the thought of lies and betrayal. His ash blond hair matted to his face thanks to the sweat and blood—so much blood. The memory flooded back.

There he stood, hand in hand with Achilles as Evora was laughing, and quite frankly, Conan couldn't remember why, but the mere sight of Evora smiling for the first time was too breathtakingly beautiful that he didn't care. For the first time, it felt like a dream.

He wasn't worrying about war, nothing about the feud between Conan's kingdom and Achilles' revolutionaries — in that moment, he felt nothing but pure love. All dreams come to an end. Most people wake up, but not Conan. God, he only *wished* he would wake up, but he couldn't. He was wide awake as he watched his living nightmare unfold around him. He was too foolish; he should've heard the whiz of the arrow, but he didn't. He watched as he saw the light leave Evora's eyes, her smile fade as blood trickled down the side of her mouth. By the time Conan noticed his army, it was too late. Three more arrows flew through the air and plunged deep into her chest. She didn't cry out, she didn't fight it, she accepted that this was her time. Conan froze in his place as Evora fell into the arms of her other brother.

"*Run*," Evora choked out, grasping onto Achilles' clothing.

"No, no, no. I'm not leaving you," Achilles cried, lowering his sister to the ground, holding her in his arms. "I promised you I wouldn't leave—I'm not going to abandon you like Mother and Father did to us, not now, not ever—"

"Achilles! We have to go!" Conan said sternly, grabbing the collar of his jacket in an attempt to pull him up, but he protested.

"No!" Achilles cried again, holding his sister to his chest. Conan could hear the stampede of the army making its way toward them, and with the mumble of a few curses under his breath, he drew Achilles' sword. They were two men against an entire army. Conan thought *maybe* he could hold them off, *maybe* he and Achilles could run off. There he stood, fighting and killing his own men, his own army in order to save the man he loved—earning himself the title of traitor to the Crown. He looked into the faces of those he grew up with, those he trained with, the men he commanded as they died by the grace of his hand. He turned as an arrow flew past his head, only to find Achilles with his sister's bow drawn, tears streaming down his face as he bared his teeth like an animal. Even the silver-plated chests of the army could not withstand the wrath of Achilles. Conan watched as his man killed an entire army in a fit of rage that he had never seen in any man before. Conan watched him stab his best friend in the chest with a broken arrow over and over again. Conan watched his lover slice his cheek with the *same* broken arrow.

Conan walked up the steps of his home in his castle. Word spreads quickly in these parts. He was face to face with his father when he walked into the castle.

"Your army. What happened?" the king demanded, without giving Conan a second to breathe.

"A revolutionary killed them all. I'm the only survivor, father," he lied through his teeth. His father arched an eyebrow with a skeptical eye as he grabbed Conan's jaw, forcibly turning his head to the side to get a good look at the cut across his cheek.

"... And this? Who gave this to you?" He pressed his thumb against the wound, making Conan flinch.

"I-uh... the revolutionary is dead. I-I'm the only survivor," he lied again.

"You keep praising the fact that only you survived. Conan, *you* are the one who is supposed to protect *your* army. They're all dead now, and you're speaking to me as if you're proud." The king raised his hand and cracked it across Conan's wounded cheek. Conan didn't flinch; he knew better than to show his weak side to his father. "You said the revolutionary is dead, correct?"

Conan stayed silent and coyly nodded, and the king's lip pursed into a sinister smile.

"Good. Bring me his head," he said in the most graceful tone as he sat upon his throne. Conan felt his stomach turn. He couldn't disappoint his father; turning up empty-handed would give away everything.

"Oh, and Conan. I hope you know that your mother would be proud of you, especially for everything you're doing for this war and to wipe out those scum revolutionaries." Conan turned and headed for the door. *Evora*. He couldn't behead Achilles, let alone kill him... but what harm would be done if he beheaded one who was already dead?

Emma Ryan, 11th Grade
Bellaire High School
(excerpted from longer piece "Occultatum")

HORATIUS
by S. E. Schneider

Rain poured down on the city of Rome. It ran off roofs and into drains. It pelted armored men, soaking their sandals. Worst of all, the rain churned the Tiber River. Water was beginning to flow out of the Tiber and onto the land. Men standing on bridges were ankle deep in water.

On the far side of the river, the side opposite Rome, an army of Etruscans marched toward the flooded bridges. It was hard to guess at their numbers through the rain, but the Plebeians who had fled to Rome claimed there were thousands. They marched on the command of the exiled king, Tarquin the Proud. The people of Rome had cast Tarquin out not long ago and now the cruel king was back to reclaim his throne.

Captain Horatius Cocles of Rome stood watching the army's progress in the relentless rain. He had faced many battles before, he had lost an eye in one battle, and he knew that Rome's only chance of survival was to let the flooded Tiber protect them. Horatius had ordered all the bridge crossings to be chopped down, and they had been. All of them except one.

"The Pons Sublicius!" cried a messenger. "The Pons Sublicius, it stands abandoned!"

Horatius cursed and ran for the bridge. It was a small, wooden structure built over the narrowest part of the river. It was no wonder it had been forgotten. Horatius sloshed up to the bridge, almost losing a sandal to the thick mud along the side of the growing river. To his dismay, he saw that the bridge was, indeed, abandoned. Or at least close to abandoned. The men who had stood guard on the bridge were running away in a panic, for bearing down on the last standing bridge were the Etruscans.

Horatius drew his sword and grabbed a fleeing man by the shoulder. "We must defend the bridge," he shouted. "Everyone! To the bridge!" To his dismay, the men continued to flee. Horatius grabbed another man, "We must keep the Etruscans at bay! Help me defend the bridge while others chop it down." The man shook free of Horatius's grasp and fled into the city. Horatius pled with the fleeing men, asking them each in turn to help him defend the city, but they all ran. When the Etruscan army was so close Horatius could hear the clinking of their armor across the water, he gave up and shouted to all who could hear, "I will defend the bridge!" He picked an axe up off the ground and tossed it to a cowering man. "If you will not defend the bridge," he growled, "then chop it down. They cannot cross into our city if there is no bridge to cross." And with that he turned and marched onto the bridge, sword and shield held high.

The water of the Tiber had risen above the level of the bridge, and it almost reached Horatius's knees. It was lucky, he thought, that the bridge was so narrow. As it was, only two men would be able to attack him at a time.

The Etruscans laughed at Horatius. How could one man stand against so many, they thought. They threw spears at Horatius, but they were a bit too far away, and his shield was a bit too quick for any damage to be done. So, with battle cries, they charged onto the bridge. Horatius stood firm and met them with the blessed courage of Mars. Every blow he struck was a killing blow; he could not afford anything else. He dealt out death as he would a deck of cards and soon the Etruscans were fighting on top of their comrades' bodies; the Tiber carried away some of the dead and left others.

A spear embedded itself into Horatius's leg and an eager sword descended upon him when he stumbled. He was saved by a friendlier sword that snaked out from behind him and parried the blow.

Two men, Spurius Lartius and Titus Herminius, had joined Horatius in the defense of the bridge. They had been assigned to watch the Pons Sublicius that day, and they had run when the Etruscans came. Now, to regain their honor, they fought beside Horatius. And they fought well; they struck like vipers from behind him and saved Horatius from many an injury.

The bridge began to shake. Horatius glanced behind him, blinking rain water out of his eyes, and saw Patricians and Plebeians alike chopping at the bridge with axes and swords. He pushed an Etruscan into the water and shouted to Herminius and Lartius, "Run! The bridge will fall soon!" They ran without hesitation. They did not want to be swept into the fury of the flooded Tiber.

Once again, Horatius stood alone. He had a dagger in his shoulder and a spear in his leg; the wounds had not been able to close because the Tiber had been steadily carrying away all his blood, but he still stood strong. The Etruscans fought with greater ferocity than before, and more of them packed onto the bridge, pressing forward. Horatius clumsily sloshed backward. Then, with one last chop from the axe of a young Plebeian boy, the bridge fell. Most of the bridge sank into the water, pulling soldiers down with it, but smaller pieces were ripped away and whipped around like misshapen spears. "Tiber protect me," Horatius prayed, as the bridge disappeared from beneath his feet and he was pulled into the Tiber.

The Tiber churned and battered Horatius. He had dropped his sword and shield. Every kick toward the surface seemed to push him farther under the water. He could no longer tell up from down. All he could see was water: water, struggling bodies and pieces of the bridge.

A strong hand gripped Horatius's arm and pulled him out of the water, onto the banks of the river. Herminius pushed Horatius onto his side. "Are you all right?" he asked. Horatius retched, bloody water coming out of his mouth and nose. He tried to push himself upright, but his hands just sank into mud. He watched the Etruscans, desperately trying to fish their comrades out of the river. They had been carried down river far away from where the Pons Sublicius had fallen. Horatius briefly wondered how Herminius had gotten far enough down river to pull him out as quickly as he did. Herminius examined the wounds on Horatius's shoulder and leg. "Someone," he called, "find a medic! He's injured!"

Horatius closed his eye and took a deep breath, trying to ignore the murmuring crowd questioning if he would live. He had bought Rome a day of respite. Right then, that was all that mattered. And so Horatius passed into legend.

Note: This is inspired by the legend of Horatius at the Bridge.

S. E. Schneider, 11th Grade
Homeschooled

LAST BREATHS
by Jacob Spann

Lilandria and Joseph sat in the dark hold of the *Cutlass*. The only lighting was the faint twinkling of stars through the window of the docking port. They heard the slight wheezing of oxygen escaping the ship, an ever-present reminder of the severity of their predicament. They faced each other, each slumped against the wall on the opposite side of the hull. Lilandria held a gun. Joseph couldn't keep his eyes off it for very long. It was a sleek, black, evil-looking instrument of death. It made him nervous. The cold, rigid metal they were leaning against began to make their backs ache. Both of them were too tired to move. Lilandria racked the gun, that one terrible note reverberating through the entire ship. The two of them were the only ones left to hear it. The air was already starting to thin.

"Okay. We've only got a few minutes left." Lilandria raised the gun to her head.

"Wait," Joseph pleaded. "Just stay. A little longer."

She said nothing but lowered the gun. Joseph half crawled, half floated over to the window. Gravity was beginning to fail inside the hold. He pressed his face right up against the immaculate glass, the sweat from his brow smearing against it. Outside, there was an infinite sea of stars. Wispy tendrils of white, running like rivers through the inky darkness of space. A few asteroids floating listlessly against the backdrop of the cosmos. Joseph thought the rocks looked very lonely. Their battered gray surfaces gave him a feeling he could somehow relate to.

As the silent ship drifted farther along its course, an eerie green light swept through the viewing port, causing Joseph and Lilandria to shield their eyes. They were approaching a cosmic maelstrom. A massive storm raged at its emerald core. The ship drifted back into a dark spot. Joseph and Lilandria lowered their arms once the pervading light had receded. Even still, impossibly bright shots of plasma lighting would shoot out of the gas cloud every now and then, lighting up their faces with haunting flashes. Metal fixtures groaned on every inch of the *Cutlass,* sending a dull echo reverberating into the hull. It was a mournful opera, sending pangs of regret through the hearts of the two doomed survivors. The ship was slowly being pulled into the gravity of the storm, causing bits of it to come loose and fly apart. That didn't matter much to the only remaining crew. The two of them would be dead long before their vessel was drawn in and torn apart by the celestial giant.

A loud humming sound that quickly faded into silence signified that the artificial gravity had gone out. Joseph began sliding away from the window, toward the ceiling. He pawed at the window, trying desperately to catch one last glimpse of the strangely beautiful force that would soon consume him. Instead, his hands made a loud wiping sound across the glass, and then his back made the soul-crushing sound of a thud against the ceiling. He floated there, pressed against the cold frame, gazing at the unnatural rays of light once again filtering into the hold. It felt like he was in a very spacious coffin with a view. Lilandria began floating upward too. She rose face up, but before she reached the ceiling she gracefully twisted in the air so that she landed gently on her back. The two watched the ethereal display of emerald beams dance and flitter on the floor. They observed in silence. Even in spite of the circumstance they thought it was quite beautiful. Joseph craned his neck to face Lilandria. She continued to look straight down. Her shoulder length brown hair was untied, and it drifted around her head as though she were under water.

"Gravity is gone. So, oxygen will be next then. I plan on using this before that happens though." She twirled the gun around her finger, almost playfully.

"Only when the oxygen goes out. Please. Promise me."

"Ok. Just don't talk that much, yeah? There's been enough talking for an entire lifetime these past weeks. I'm quite honestly sick to death of it."

"I'll try I guess. There's nothing you want to say to me though? I mean, we are about to die together."

"Why should that matter? I didn't even know you until a few days ago."

"What the hell are you saying? I've known you since we were kids, Lilandria."

"You knew of me, sure. But c'mon. We didn't know each other. We still don't really. We just happened to be recruited for the same assignment aboard the *Cutlass*. I would see you sometimes on the colony and at school, and when we graduated sometimes you'd drive past my AgriSquare, and if you'd looked you would've seen me toiling away on my little plot of alien dirt. There's not really much of a chance you won't see anyone more than once on a colony. But we never talked, did we? Why should now be any different?"

Joseph tried to speak but his voice cracked and he sputtered out something unintelligible. He took a deep breath and regained his composure. "It should be different now. It should be, probably because we're about to die. I don't want to spend my last moments in utter silence when there's a perfectly good person by me to speak to! Seriously, find some compassion!"

"A perfectly good person to speak to," she repeated. There was animosity on her tongue. "I wish you'd felt that way before we were about to die. Before we got on this ship."

Joseph was about to speak again, but the entire hold began to shudder with an intensity previously unfamiliar to the two. After their surroundings stabilized, their bodies began to slide toward the wall on the left. Joseph hit the corner first with Lilandria piling on top of him.

"There," he said. "That is a much more agreeable attitude to be having."

She planted her feet in his stomach then, pushing off his body toward the other side of the room. Gravity would pull her back, so she grabbed hold of a pipe snaking down the right wall. She floated in the room completely horizontally, her feet dangling in Joseph's direction.

"What is your problem?!" Joseph rasped when he recaptured his breath.

"No problem. I just don't see why we need to be so chummy all of a sudden."

"Maybe you don't recall, but when those things ate most of our crew and then tore apart the ship, I saved your life by dragging you in here! So maybe you could indulge me given the circumstance. All I want is to have someone to talk to before the end."

"You speak as if you've done me some favor! We're going to die in here too! I least before I could have died while unconscious! Well it seems like you're already getting what you want. Despite my previous request. It's honestly incredible. Even now, men are still getting what they want at the expense of women."

"Oh, don't start that bullshit with me! We are about to die, lady! And you're talking about male privilege?!"

Lilandria did her best to sweep her floating hair out of the way. She craned her neck to look at her crew mate. Her left arm was beginning to hurt from fighting the pull of gravity. "I just think it's funny. That's all." Her tone was calm and even. This just pissed Joseph off even more.

"You are a piece of work. It's no wonder I never spoke to you back at the colony! I just want someone to speak to before my life ends forever. But no! Now I'm some misogynist villain! Now I'm some burden!" His face became ashen, and then he whispered in a meek voice, "Oh god. We're about to die."

The two floated in silence for a few minutes. The light from outside was raging brighter and brighter. The pair could see each other quite clearly now. Silent tears drifted out of Joseph's eyes and began to be pushed into small pools around his head. Lilandria saw this and gazed at him incredulously. Nevertheless, she let go of the pipe she'd been clinging to and floated back to reside next to her conversation partner. They were fated to die here, she thought. Brought together by some sort of design or dumb luck. So, she resolved to do one last good thing with what she had been given.

"You're right. I shouldn't be so difficult. What is ill will going to accomplish now anyway?" Her words had softened, but her tone was still slightly detached.

"Now how come that was so hard to admit?" he said.

"Because I resented you, I guess. You were part of a big shot military family on the colony. I came from nothing. We lived very separate lives, even though we shared the same relatively confined space of the colony. I had to work hard to get where I am. It was a huge deal when I had made enough credit to buy my way onto this expedition and off the colony. You were literally born to be on this detail."

"Yeah, all the good it's done me. Having an Admiral as a father has its ups and downs. I never even wanted to come on this little wonder cruise, but Dad thought it'd toughen me up or something. I'm a grown man and he still strong-armed me. I don't know why I let him, the bastard."

"You still get the point. I guess I was just mad. You've never had a reason to give a rat's ass about me, and now here we are. Having never spoken a full sentence to each other until a few days ago, even though we've seen each other almost every day since we were five years old. But none of that matters now. I don't want to talk about any of that. What do you want to say? You can vent more about your dad if you want."

Joseph waved his hand dismissively. "Eh, the guy's a tool. What more is there to say?" When the silence began to drag again, he suddenly broke out into an impression of his old man. "Stand at attention! Fire on my command! Plunder these new worlds! God bless humanity, and God bless America!"

Lilandria giggled. "That's actually pretty good."

Joseph maintained his rigid pose and stiff lip. "Did I give you permission to address me, crewman?! And that's actually pretty good, *Sir*. Don't forget the sir."

"All right, now you're pushing it," she said, still grinning from ear to ear.

He went to open his mouth to reply. No sound came out. A look of wild confusion passed over his face, but it was gone in seconds. A fear more intense than anything Lilandria had ever witnessed entered his eyes. A desperate impulse from the brain to stay alive, even though no hope of survival existed. The oxygen had finally gone out in the hold. The searing emerald light from the window spiked suddenly, becoming so bright that all they could see was each other. Lilandria looked at Joseph with all the calm she could muster. She nodded, as if to say it was all going to be okay. Her sweaty hand clutched the gun fiercely, her knuckles whitening from the strain. She placed the barrel on Joseph's forehead. Globs of liquid swirled around his eyes. She wiped them so he could see her. She mouthed a message to him. *Let's talk more sometime.* Then she pulled the trigger. Droplets of blood and chunks of wet brain floated onto her face and body. More remains swirled but a few inches in front of her, and then were gone out of sight, absorbed by the blistering brightness. Joseph's corpse disappeared as well. Something smelled burned inside the hull, and Lilandria realized it was her skin. Without another thought, she turned the weapon on herself.

Hours later the hold was torn apart by a massive stray bolt of energy from the maelstrom ripping through it. Everything inside was disintegrated in a flash of brilliant green heat, leaving no trace of the two lives that had run parallel for so long, and had finally been connected by their last breaths.

Jacob Spann, 11th Grade
Traverse City Central

ELLE
by Molly Stadler

I take a deep breath. It's a little past midnight, but I'm not tired. I've been staying up late lately. It's been a few days since we have talked, and you made it abundantly clear that you don't want to anymore. I want to. I want you.

It's not my choice though, and I respect your decision. I just –I just miss you. My index finger hovers over the photos app on my cell phone and I don't know if I can bear seeing your face again. All of the photos have already been taken off my walls. They're bare now. A sterile white, aside from my aunt Cindy's art. I wish I could just get you out of my head, but it's gotten so bad that I can see your face in the abstract shapes on every canvas in the room. It's rough, to say the very least.

I have to go through with this. I can't keep pretending that everything will just suddenly go back to normal. I flick my index finger against the screen and the squares flash and spin and blend together in a Russian roulette of heartbreak. Which few frames will we stop on?

June 12 of 2017, apparently. It says so in black lettering above the photo as I click on it. There are flowers in your hair. I remember I plucked them, illegally, off the bushes in the state park. Your hair was blue then. Pastel blue, a little paler than a cloudless sky.

My mouth goes dry. I can feel cotton balls being forced inside of it and –I remember. That was our anniversary. One year. You had surprised me with a picnic under the trees. That was the reason you hadn't texted me the night before. You were busy in the kitchen making those god-awful—but I would never tell you that—sandwiches and trying to plan that day for us. I can't apologize for getting mad now. I should've then, because maybe that is what triggered it. I mean, your disdain for me. Maybe that's what caused a strain on our relationship, me being an asshole because I wasn't getting enough attention. God, I'm pathetic. I press my finger against the little blue trash can icon, and I want to punch a wall and I want to cry because this is all my fault.

I swipe left to see the next photo of you. May 1, 2017. It was that time we went to see the northern lights. They were faint that night. Almost like a soft green smoke pluming up over the waves and along the horizon. We ended up paying more attention to the stars, laying our backs against the seagrass, wet sand clinging to our sweatshirts, and your hand holding onto mine for warmth. I remember you snuggling up closer to me. Your parents were too preoccupied with the fact that your siblings were having a sand fight. It seemed like it was just you and me and the universe that night.

I click delete and I crack my knuckles. Then I crack my neck and stretch and clench my jaw because this is a mess, and it's too hard to relive all of our memories when you're not here.

I continue scrolling past dead memes and Spotify screenshots of songs I recommended to Jamie and my other friends until I see a photo of a text from you. April 16, 2017. It was the first time you told me you loved me. I can't take this anymore. I click the select button and drag my finger to the top covering every photo in my library with a blue check mark.

I switch apps over to Instagram and scroll through my home page. It's full of memes that I saw three days ago on Reddit, and none of them are remotely funny. I keep swiping up at the screen and reloading the page hoping for something interesting, but the only thing that appears when I load the page is a photo of you and your friends and me captioned, "I love you guys." I furrow my eyebrows, confused as to why you're posting me when you just told me you didn't want me anymore. Rather than wallow in my confusion and bitterness, I decide to shoot you a message. I switch over to IMessage because it's way too cringey to try to win back your girl in an Instagram DM. I type out, "I miss you," and immediately erase it because what am I thinking? If I did that I'd get a *read 5 minutes ago* receipt with no reply. Ever.

I punch out a "Can we talk?" instead because you're way more likely to respond to a message if it's a question, and then I throw my phone across my bed.

A minute later I hear the phone buzz. I grab my phone in the fastest motion possible and hold my thumb to the home button. My phone vibrates and reads, "Try Again." I punch in my number quickly, only to click on my messages and see that the notification was from Jennifer, the admissions assistant at Augustana College, letting me know about scholarship opportunities. I close my eyes and groan as my phone dings again.

It's a text from Elle. You. I click on the message and it reads, "I'm sorry. I overreacted. I miss you. I'll Facetime you later, and we can talk about everything. I'm sorry. I still love you."

I break down. I told myself this whole time that I wouldn't cry, but I am. It's not even because I'm sad. At this point, this sense of relief I feel is so powerful that I can't feel any other emotions. I cry for about a minute until I remember that I need to text you back before you think I'm a jerk who was just wondering why you just posted me.

I type back an "Okay. Can't wait," and toss my phone near my pillow. I lie on my bed, statue-still, and wait for your call.

Molly Stadler, 12th Grade
Grand Traverse Academy

ANXIETY
by Calista Trowbridge

I can't explain it—if I try, I end up speechless
The choking-like sensation that sits in my throat gets bigger with every breath
Holding back a tsunami of tears with a painted smile
It tells me that I'm a mistake,
That I should have been aborted,
That I'm just a waste of air.
I'm not lazy.
I'm lying in bed fighting with my own thoughts,
It tells me that I'm going to fail today so why bother getting up?
I'm not stupid.
I try to get my work done but it will remind me of an awkward conversation I had years ago and take my motivation away.
My thoughts fight me every day pointing a gun at my head
Some days there's a bullet and some there isn't,
I'm not anorexic.
I eat but it tells me that I'm a disappointment to not only myself but to my family
I'm scared.
I'm scared that one day, I'm going to lose control.

That one day, I'll go back to slicing up my skin.
That one day, I'll never achieve my goals.
That one day, I'll never be able to breathe again.
That one day, I'll never be happy.
I fight with my mind so much it leaves me tired
I'm seen as happy and confident.
But talk about my feelings I'm emotional and weak
My emotions make me fall to my knees crying my eyes out,
I hate to be seen as weak because I'll never get the same respect
    I had before.
When I walk through the halls I feel like everyone is looking at
    me, judging me
Making fun of what I wear, my personality, my skin tone, my laugh.
Oh, and let's not forget: oh my god she's a virgin!
It reminds me of my insecurities.
It reminds me to look in the mirror and criticize myself
I hate that it's here.
I hate that it sits on its throne that I call my mind,
I hate that it makes me shake like a rattlesnake's tail,
People tell me to calm down – you telling me to calm down isn't
    going to help.
I already feel like I'm drowning and your words make me sink
    deeper,
Making me regret telling you about my illness in the first place
I can't explain it if I try. I'm speechless but I can say this
It's like a demon feeding off your happiness and replacing it with
    your insecurities.

Calista Trowbridge, 12th Grade
TC West Senior High

LATE NIGHT CIGARETTES
by Adam Warner

CAST OF CHARACTERS

ASH   17 years old. Cares about friends and sister. Lives in loft above bar.

WILL   18 years old. New to town. Smoker. Lives near a park.

Scene
Small town in Oregon.

Time
2 a.m. in the morning, present day. October.

Scene 1

AT RISE: Outside a gas station at 2 a.m.

Small town, Oregon.

ASH is chilling on the edge of the sidewalk.

WILL is leaving the gas station, opening a pack of cigarettes.

WILL

Do you have a lighter?

(ASH looks up with a sarcastic grin)

ASH
Don't you know smoking is bad for you?

WILL (Grinning)
Actually, I didn't but thank you for changing my life.

ASH (laughing)
No problem.

WILL
So, no lighter?

ASH
No.

WILL (disappointed)
Darn it.

ASH
Yeah I know, I've been disappointing people my whole life. Ya get used to it.

WILL
Wow. So, what's going on with you?

ASH
What makes you think something's wrong? The fact that I wasn't nice to a stranger at 1 a.m.?

WILL
2 a.m.

ASH (Slightly annoyed yet alarmed)
What?

WILL
It's 2 a.m.

ASH
Didn't your mother ever tell you that it's rude to correct strangers?
(Will looks down at his shoes)

WILL (Taken aback)
No. she ... uhh ... never got the chance to.

ASH (Sympathetic)
Oh. I'm sorry.

WILL
It's whatever, I never got to know her anyway.

ASH
Oh.

WILL
You never answered my question.

ASH
Huh?

WILL
I asked you what was wrong. Because you don't see a lot of teenagers sitting on a sidewalk alone at 2 a.m. So, either you're depressed or you're homeless. So ...

ASH (Irritated)
Do I look homeless to you?

WILL (Tripping over his words)
WHAT?! NO! I was just trying to be funny.

ASH (laughing)
I know.
WILL
So then why are you here?

ASH
Because where else am I supposed to be?

WILL
I don't know. Maybe ... home?

ASH
Maybe you're right.

(ASH pauses and pulls out his phone. It's dead)

ASH
Hey, what time is it now?

WILL
2:15 a.m.

ASH (Sarcastic yet serious)
Okay. Well then, I think I should go home.

WILL
Just like that?

ASH
Just like that.

(ASH starts to walk away, exiting the gas station parking lot and onto the sidewalk.)

SCENE 2

AT RISE: ASH is walking home. The sidewalk is illuminated by street lamps. Loud footsteps can be heard behind him. Almost like someone is running. ASH, alarmed, turns around to see WILL running after him trying to catch up.

ASH
(Alarmed) (Out of breath)
What are you doing?!
Are you following me?
'Cause dude like why would you run after me? That's pretty stalkerish. So, what's up? Why are you here?

WILL
So that's it. You're just going home? Without giving me your name or anything? I thought we had some type of connection or something. Well, maybe not a strong connection, but I thought you were cool and I don't know, but... Actually, if I freaked you out, I'm so sorry. That was not my intention.

ASH
You don't have to be sorry.

WILL
I don't?

ASH
Nope. But seriously, what are you doing here?

WILL
Do you mean like what am I doing in the universe? Or do you mean on this sidewalk? That's a loaded question, man.

ASH
The sidewalk.

WILL
I'm walking you home.

ASH (Doubtful)
You're gonna walk me home?

WILL (Grinning)
Hopefully.

ASH

You don't know where I live! You literally met me 30 minutes ago. You don't even know my name, or anything about me.

WILL

Exactly.

ASH (Jokingly)

You're not a murderer, are you?

WILL

Why would I be a murderer?

ASH

Because it's not every day strangers from gas stations want to walk me home.

WILL

If I wanted to kill you I would've done it already.

ASH

So why do you want to walk a stranger home? What if I'm the killer? Why would I let a stranger follow me?

WILL

My name's Will.

ASH

What?

WILL

That's my name, Will.

ASH (Weary)

My name's Ashton, but everyone calls me Ash.

WILL

Pleasure to meet you, Ash.

ASH (Grinning)

You too.

(They both start to walk together.)

WILL

So. What school do you go to?

ASH

Westbank High.

WILL

Oh, well, as of tomorrow so will I.

ASH

Oh, really? Well, then I'm sorry for your loss.

WILL

That bad? What's it like?

ASH

You know Hogwarts?

WILL

Yeah.

ASH

It's like that, only no magic, no castle, no Harry Potter, nothing fun or magical, ya know.

WILL

Oh, so it's nothing like Hogwarts.

ASH

Yeah, basically.

WILL

Oof.

ASH (Sarcastically)
Don't worry though. I'm sure you'll love it.

WILL (Worried)
Ha-ha, yeah...

ASH
Anyways, what brings you here? I've never seen you here before, and I know it wasn't to meet gas station strangers at 2 a.m.

WILL
Did you just basically ask me if I come here often?

ASH
Oof, I guess I did. How cliché.
(They stop walking. There's a pause of awkward silence.)

WILL
Do you believe in destiny?

ASH
What did you just ask me?

WILL
You know, two strangers meet late at night. This could be the gods giving us a sign!

ASH (Confused)
The gods?

WILL
Yes, the gods. Do you not believe in God?

ASH (sighing)
I believe that I make my own path. Too much bad stuff has gone on in my life for some "god" to be real.

WILL
Like what?

ASH
None of your business.

WILL
Oh.

ASH
Yeah.

(They start walking again)

WILL
You didn't answer my question.

ASH
What question?

WILL
What do you think that two people must have in common to connect?

ASH
Oh, uhh, I never really thought about that.

WILL (Sarcastically amazed)
Wow.

ASH
Well, what do you think? It was your question.

WILL
I don't know, man. Sometimes we are just putting out them vibes into the universe that bond us. Maybe it was the universe that wants us to meet.

ASH

Oh, so now it's the universe that wants us to meet?

WILL

Precisely.

ASH

Okay, man.

WILL (Self-consciously)

Are you judging me?

ASH

What? No. I just thought your answer was interesting. So why do you ask?

WILL

Oh. That's easy. It's a good question to ask people when you meet.

ASH

Why?

WILL

Because it helps to get a better feel of who they are.

ASH

I see.

WILL

Yeah.

ASH

So... did you get a better feel of who I am? Based off that one question?

WILL (smiling.)

I think so.

SCENE 3

>AT RISE: ASH and WILL are walking through town.
>
>They approach a bar with a yellow neon sign labeled *The Trophy Room*. Music can be heard from behind the doors.
>
>ASH stops in front of the bar and gestures his arms at the door.

>>ASH

Here we are!

>>WILL

At a bar?

>(ASH points at the second floor of the building)

>>ASH

No. I live up there. My sister owns the bar. I live with her.

>>WILL

Really? That's cool! What do your parents think?

>(WILL and ASH sit on the curb in front of the bar)

>>ASH

They were not thrilled. According to them it was "Jae's biggest mistake." They tried to kick her out. And I objected. So, they told me to leave too.

>>WILL

D—.

>>ASH

Yeah, but it's fine. It was two years ago. My sister and I are happy here. Plus, in this town I made some pretty great friends.

>>WILL

Did you meet them at gas stations too?

ASH (Grinning)
Sadly not.

WILL
Cool. So that makes me special?

ASH
Well I don't normally let strangers walk me home, so I guess.

WILL
So, I guess this is goodbye.

ASH
I guess it is.

WILL
So, I guess I will see you tomorrow? At school?

ASH
Yeah. Goodnight.
> (ASH starts to walk inside.)

WILL
WAIT ASH!
> (ASH opens the door and looks at WILL)

ASH
Yeah?

WILL
I didn't get your number?! How will I see you again?!

ASH
Guess you'll have to talk to me in person then. Walk me to school tomorrow?

                    WILL (Grinning)
Really? I'd like that.

                    (End of scene)
                    (End of play)

Adam Warner, 11th Grade
Forest Area High School

THE GIRL IN THE BACK CORNER
by Dominque Williams

I stare up at the girl who faces the window
Blankly staring at the rain that dots the other side
I can hear her music that continuously blares in her ears
She slowly takes her hand from under her chin
And looks at the bright screen behind me before picking me up and taking a sip
It feels like forever to me as I begin to study her face from a different perspective
The dark circles that hug her eyes tightly,
The little freckles that lightly spread over parts of her softly shaped face,
The patches of acne on her forehead and cheeks,
Her short, curled eyelashes,
Her long, untamed hair, pulled into a messy bun
I feel her soft, warm hands hold my sides and am at peace
But as quick as it started, it was gone
She sighed contentedly as she put me down
And left me with the heat of what was a drink and nothing else.

Dominque Williams, 11th Grade
Traverse City Central High School

BAD DREAM
by Dominque Williams

She aches in pain as she slowly limps
Sinking more and more into the snow with every step
Frightened of what fate may serve to her next
She hears a loud screech from miles away
And starts to run
But falls after the first stride
And cries out for someone to help her up
As she lies on her stomach, she continues to sob
She looks toward the sky
And apologizes for everything she's done
As the screeches get louder and the footsteps come closer
She shuts her eyes and waits for her demise
But all that's waiting for her when she opens them
Is the sound of her clock softly ticking and the purring of her cats that lie on her bed
She jerks up, waking her cats, and gasps for breath
Feeling her side where just a minute ago was a bleeding wound
But is now her baggy shirt slightly damp from sweat
She takes one last look around her room before lying back down
And shuts her eyes once more
"Just a bad dream."

Dominque Williams, 11th Grade
Traverse City Central High School

THE PRINCE OF FIRE AND ICE
by David Yuhaus

I didn't think that I would be able to be in the light ever again, consumed by darkness twenty-four hours a day, except for the small moments when the slot in the door opened and food spilled out in a heap of mixed messes. Sometimes I could see what it might be, but others, it had turned to mush. Globs of slop that were warm in some spots and cold in others, giving a sensation that was unlike anything that I had felt in my time in the palace. I spent most of my time huddled in a corner, trying to keep warm. The metal walls were always so cold, yet when I sat up against them for long enough, they could become warm. Every time that a meal was served, I was bathed in light, making it seem as though a fraction of the sun were sent through, blinding me for several moments, but when the spots faded, a plate of food was left. Sometimes a miracle occurred, and the plate was completely right side up, but on a normal day it was upside-down and had bugs crawling in it. You know how far you have fallen when your only competitors are beetles. I could only hold the fond memories of when I was considered royalty. I was the one everyone wanted to be, the lone soul who was envied throughout the world. Little did they know, they were all wrong, and in a way, I had fallen farther than they could ever know.

Today was no different from any other day. I woke to find a room, if you could even call it that, so dark I couldn't tell if I was truly awake. So dark, I started to see things in my sight; pigments of green and blue moved across my vision, in a synchronized dance until they decided to move on and leave me to my increasing insanity. I figured my food was going to be coming soon, so I positioned myself in front of the door to catch it before it clattered onto the floor, only for the real door to open to my right, blinding me once again and spilling cold oatmeal all over me. It seemed to be too hard to be edible. I picked up what I could salvage from the bowl, which wasn't much. I scarfed down the disgusting lumps of oats that seemed to collect in my teeth more than down my throat. I had just finished and thrown my tray onto the mountain of trays that the guards never seemed to pick up when I heard a bang that rattled the steel box in which I was kept. I leaned into the door and listened. The sound of clicks and clanks were just beyond the door, and suddenly, my cell door was opening, screeching against the stone door frame. After over a year in prison, I was finally able to see the sky again, and even though it was night it felt as though my eyes were being burned from the light. My contentment was short-lived because after I was done allowing my eyes to adjust, a guard ran past my cell to see me sitting there. He seemed to be furious and wanted to take it all out on me. He was overweight and inexperienced. This was my first opponent in my grand escape, and it definitely wasn't going to be my last. I stepped toward him as he ran at me, and right before he was ready to swing, I jabbed my foot into his back foot, and used his own momentum to carry him over my back and sprawling down onto the floor behind me. Even from that small move, I'd already felt winded, out of breath and out of shape. These prison cells were meant to break you and make you believe that there was no hope for escape or salvation. This should have been true of course, but here I was outside my cell and ready to get out of this place any way I could.

I progressed through the halls to see cells in other wings had been opened with prisoners running amok and ransacking unconscious guards. I couldn't help hoping for a release issued by my father, but I knew that he would never let out these traitors and psychopaths, not to mention he would never want to see me after what I had done. I stayed low and against the nearby wall trying to close off any potential sightlines for any guards who had not been taken out yet. I needed to stay out of sight as much as possible because if the guards found me, I would be put back in a cell even worse than the last, but if any of the prisoners found me, I knew I would be dead.

I soon realized my foul stench and even worse physique. I had been reduced to a skinny, pale, bony boy who you might have seen lining the road after a raid. I progressed to the main door, and as I looked around the final corner to my escape, there was another party waiting there: my brother, Lau, the one who had abandoned me at the Battle of the Final Days.

I swore a long time ago that I would kill him, but now that he was standing in front of me, I was hesitant. I decided at that point that it would have been unwise to attack. I wasn't at my best and he could definitely overpower me if I tried to attack directly. Given my luck, that moment was when Lau decided to look behind him and in doing so, caused me to reel back so quickly I could feel the strain in my neck. I heard his footsteps closing the distance between us quickly, so I turned and ran until I heard something from him that made me stop.

"Lee?" he said stopping in his tracks, "I thought you were dead."

"Well, as you can see, I'm not," I said bitterly. "Sorry to ruin your plans, your highness."

"What are you talking about, I tried to find you for months after the battle," he said in a voice absorbed in regret. "I came here trying to break out other prisoners of war, but I had no idea that you were here. I am so sorry."

I hesitated at this.

"Well, you weren't here to break me out so you might want to keep to your objective," I said turning around. "It was always something you were good at."

"I didn't know you were here. If I did, there would have been no way I wouldn't have come for you," he said desperately. "We interrogated everyone after you were captured to try to find you—"

"Obviously not," I snapped, turning around. "I was left to die, by *you*." I locked eyes with him and jabbed his chest. I could feel my hands tingling with rage and bitterness, emotions that I had kept bottled up for far too long.

"What are talking about?" he said so innocently that I wanted to throttle the life from his bulky frame.

"What am *I* talking about? I'm talking about when you left me behind, beaten and bloodied by *our father* and left without even looking back," I said in a yell, now steaming with anger. It was at this point that I didn't care if the guards had found where I was; this was my time to get my rage out of my system.

"We didn't do any of that, I prom-" he started.

"You *promise*? I remember the last time you promised something—the time when we were about to assault the palace, the last time I saw your face without wanting to stab a knife through it. You left me to *die*! The only thing you wanted was an empty path to the throne," I yelled back. "You're nothing to me and you shall never be again." I then turned away, raising the hood of the robe I'd stolen, running down the hall ignoring the yelling of my former brother in the background. I ran until I found the way Lau had come through. As guards came to me, I beat them into walls and threw them over ledges into masses of escapees. Some of them weren't even there to stop me; they were just trying to desert and avoid persecution by the escaped prisoners, and I escaped the place that had kept me for so long. I was finally free.

The first thing I vowed to do was get new clothes and take a bath. I stank worse than anything I ever smelled. I wore what remained of my old battle uniform, worn during the siege, under my new robe. I had taken the robe from a fallen guard to provide some warmth to the bleak and unforgiving Northern Mountains. Few could remember when this wasn't controlled by my father's tyranny, but the remains of the mountainside villages were constant reminders of what had been, and what was now. I wandered through the remains of an old village—houses crumbled, once magnificent buildings of glory and honor stripped away to mossy walls and cracked floors. Bodies littered the streets, the ground still stained crimson with blood, the screams of the dead still frozen on their withered forms. Pacing through the town made me see what my father was capable of. I headed into a house that was mostly intact. I went in, seeing family photos caked with dirt and dust. I looked for a bath and prayed for some running water so I could bathe. I got lucky that there was a functioning faucet in one of the tubs, but the water seemed as if it could have been laced with ice. I looked around the house as the tub filled, finding some rocks and pieces of metal, hoping that I could start a fire. I went outside and found some mostly dry things in the leaves, some wood that was kept dry from some rubble next to the remains of a storage house. I brought it in and set it under the tub. If it did light, I wouldn't have a whole lot of time before it got uncomfortable. It wouldn't burn hot, or for very long, but it just might do the trick and get me somewhat cleaner. I struck each rock with each piece of metal and after many tries it finally worked, letting out a small flame that danced below the basin. I removed my tattered clothes and lowered myself into the tub. I was still chilled to the bone, even with the fire, but it definitely helped. After a while, I could feel the warmth within the water spreading to each corner of the bath, but it wasn't going to last, so I got out and dried myself with the robe and went around looking for a change of clothes. I found some upstairs that fit me quite well and another more formal robe that seemed more my speed. I found everything I needed, a green shirt with brown trim and gray pants with a red velvet robe that was lined with sheep's wool that could keep me warm outside. I set them all out beside the bed upstairs and collapsed on top of it. I expected to feel relieved, but I felt something else. It felt, *abnormal*. Like it was *too* soft as it was made of clouds and from some illusion, but it must have been made from an illusion that I could live with because I crashed almost instantly.

David Yuhaus, 11th Grade
Bellaire

NMC CREATIVE WRITING WORKSHOPS

LOST IN MYSELF
by Cici Copenhaver

Tween Writer's Machine
Instructor: Claire Alexander

It is hard to put what I want to say into words, because wouldn't it be easier to speak in feelings? Words have no purpose; they just create walls between races and make it almost impossible to express ourselves. All should speak the same language, a language that binds us to form one. Not two or three or four, but one.

I sit in my car. It is the fifth of March and the air is bitter with a hint of sweetness. March is the time when we yearn for spring, but end up getting only a taste of it and having to wait a whole month before it arrives. These are the thoughts that I ponder as I drive to the O'Hare Airport in Chicago. My destination: Hawaii. That is where my history is, where the rich culture that I come from stands. However, I was born in Chicago and have never explored my past. My curly, dark brown hair bounces in front of my eyes, making it hard to see. I tie it back and realize that I need to turn left in one mile in order to reach the airport. Putting on my signal, I turn onto the exit.

My stomach cries for mercy as I zip down the road. I stop to get a snack at a pizza place. I walk in the door, a small bell tinkling as I step inside.

"Seat yourself," a gruff voice says as I look around.

"Thank you," I reply, taking a seat in a small booth on the right side of the room.

"A slice of pepperoni, please," I tell the waiter, grinning.

As I'm looking down on my phone, a thought flies through my head. Will she accept me? I'm so different from her. Our ways are like mismatched puzzle pieces, wanting to click but simply can't. The song that I haven't heard of she still sings. I'm so lost. I don't know how we're cousins.

"Sometimes you have to be lost to find yourself." I look up staring into two bright green eyes. An elderly woman carries my pizza, a mysterious smile playing at her lips. "Where are you headed?" she asks, sitting down on the booth across from me.

"Oh... uh, H-Hawaii." I am so startled by her appearance, the words get lost. See, this is why I hate words.

"Ahh, Hawaii. So why are you so nervous?"

I shake my head. "I... um."

"No, no sweetie," she interrupts me, "I don't need to know why. I just wanted to know how."

With that she gets up from the leather seat, winks and hobbles off.

This leaves me shocked and curious. "How." What did she mean by that? I sigh and look at my phone hoping for a text from my cousin. Instead, I'm met with the time. 3:38. My flight leaves in an hour. Blood rushes to me head as I stand up suddenly, leave money on the table and run to my car. I don't think I've ever driven so fast. I feel like air is under me as I speed toward the airport. Breathing heavily, I rush through security and am desperate to get to my section. Luckily, I make it just in time.

As I board the airplane, a sudden calmness settles over my

body. I made it. Sinking into my seat, I put my buckle on and listen to the flight attendant announce things over the intercom.

"This will be a 13-hour flight," she says, "so make sure to sit back and relax."

Just then, I get a text from my cousin. "Can't wait 2 see U soon! We are going to have so much fun!" Leaning back in my seat, I grinned. I would finally get to meet my relatives and unearth my history. I would meet someone who is like me and no longer feel left out. If I could describe how excited I am in words, I would. But sometimes, the only way to talk is through your emotions. And if there were one word to describe my emotions right now, it would be happy.

To be continued...

Cici Copenhaver
Traverse City West Middle School, 7th Grade

DELPHI – A CURSED CHILD PREQUEL (EXCERPT)

By Gabrielle Parker

Hogwarts School of Wizardry and Writing
Instructor: Shannon McCann

Chapter 4: Delphi Grows Up

(One month after Delphi's 22nd birthday)

Leaves and twigs snapped and crackled underneath Delphi's shoes as she made her way through the woods. Earlier that day, Euphemia [her foster mother] died from old age. To say that Delphi was sad would be like saying that the sky was pink. But either way, she just needed to take a walk.

All of a sudden, someone grabbed her by the arm and pulled her into some nearby bushes. Delphi shoved her assailant away to see what he looked like, and he was an absolute wreck.

"Who are you?!" hissed Delphi furiously. "You look like you just escaped from Azkaban, you lunatic!"

The man cackled insanely, causing Delphi to flinch back.

"Th-that's because I just did!" His fingers trembled with excitement. "Oh my, last time I saw you, you were this big!" He held up two fingers about four inches apart from each other to demonstrate.

"Your point being?" Delphi snapped.

"Delphini...did Euphemia Rowle ever tell you who your parents are?"

Delphi gave him a suspicious glare.

"No. I never knew my father or my mother."

The man put one hand to his thin chest and explained. "I am Rudolphus Lestrange. You know, the one who was paying Euphemia from Azkaban. And...well, guess what? I'll tell you who your parents are! Right now!! At this very moment! Your father is Lord Voldemort, and your mother is Bellatrix Lestrange!!"

For a moment, everything seemed to freeze in time. Sure, Delphi had no reason to believe this crazy old man, but it all made so much sense. Her ability with spells. Her inability to feel love. Her hatred for everything. Mortimer, the imaginary friend who looked like Voldemort. It all added up. She was Voldemort's daughter!

Rudolphus snapped Delphi out of her thoughts by saying, "My dear Delphini."

He grabbed her hands and looked into her milky blue eyes.

"You must finish what your father started. Now that he is gone, are the heir of Salazar Slytherin. You must start by erasing everyone's memory in this village." Suddenly they both heard a voice.

"What is this?! Who are you?!"

A voice that sounded like shattering icicles cut through the air like a knife. Delphi and Rudolphus whirled around to see Scipio, a now very handsome young man of twenty-nine years, standing angrily with his arms crossed over his chest.

"Who do you think you are, tramp!" he swore. "Telling Delphi she's Voldemort's offspring and that she has to obliviate everyone! Nonsense! Scram!"

A blast of ice shot from Scipio's hands and toward Rudolphus. He howled in terror at the wintry phenomenon and bolted off at the speed of light, leaving just Delphi and Scipio.

"Delphi," whispered Scipio.

Delphi almost laughed at how the tone of his voice changed so quickly. Could all magical ice beings do that?

"You don't...actually believe him, do you?"

If looks could kill, the one that Delphi gave Scipio in that moment would instantly do the job.

"Yes," she growled. "I do. All the puzzle pieces match up, Scipio. And if you're going to go against me, then I'll...." She held up her wand. "...have to kill you. And I will get away with all of this. Avada kedav ... "

Scipio held his hands above his head, and with the coldest glare on his face that Delphi had ever received from anyone, uttered four final words to her: "No, Delphi. You won't." And with the icy swirl of a mini blizzard, he was gone.

To be continued in "Harry Potter and the Cursed Child"

Gabrielle "Gabi" Parker
St. John Paul II, 9th Grade, Avondale, Arizona

WHAT'S AROUND US
By Nora Riley

Writing and Publishing: Finding Your Voice
Instructor: Kevin Fitton

She felt ditched. She, Sarah Spellberg, the girl whose parents never left her side, had been ditched at her grandfather's house. Sarah never thought these dreadful events would occur, but yet here she was, waiting by Grandpa Morrie's mailbox. Her parents had dropped her off ever so randomly, and it simply ticked her off. She understood that every parent needed a break from their child, especially when those parents had been given first-class tickets to Hawaii, by their "ever so generous boss."

Sarah had told her parents that mixing business with pleasure was a terrible idea, but nonetheless here she was. Waiting for her grandpa to get flour to make pancakes. Waiting for him to get back from the grocery store. It was 1:30, and she was starved to death. Crazy old man. Heartless mom and dad. These were her only thoughts, pounding in her head. She knew that her parents had gone away to Stuart, Florida, just to have a little time for themselves. Although she understood their need to escape, she still felt as if the entire situation was painfully unfair. "Stupid, stupid, stupid," she mumbled to herself.

Suddenly, an old Chevy pickup entered the driveway.

"Grandpa, finally," she thought.

Grandpa Morrie stepped out of the truck, his leather shoes shining in the sun. He was holding a box of Betty Crocker dry ingredients and a carton of organic milk.

"Hello, Sarah!"

"Hey, Grandpa," Sarah said under her breath.

He had not even apologized for taking so long to pick up the ingredients. She wondered if he was of sound mind, considering the fact that he was eighty-six years old and often forgot what day it was. They walked up the narrow, gravel driveway together and entered Grandpa Morrie's fishing hut, or rather his home.

Sarah liked to think of it as a fishing hut since it was incredibly small.

"What an absolute inconvenience," she thought to herself.

Sarah's home wasn't a mansion, but it was certainly spacious, unlike Grandpa's hut. She knew that Grandpa had plenty of money before he downsized, but she wasn't sure what happened to all of it. It was as if his riches had vanished into thin air, along with so many of the other things she remembered about him—his constant need for the most scrumptious sweets and his incessant chatter about politics. Grandpa seemed quieter now and slightly sullen. But perhaps there had always been a misunderstanding between the two of them.

If Sarah were to look on the bright side of the situation, she should be grateful for Grandpa Morrie's pancakes and approach her time with him as an opportunity to get to know him better. The pancakes were chocolate-raspberry monster pancakes, topped with whipped cream and honey. The perfect way to start your day ... at 1:30 in the afternoon. And Grandpa Morrie's wisdom could certainly teach Sarah something about the natural world and the most recent environmental protests that had been happening throughout the town surrounding Lake MacGregor.

Instead, she chose to think of her time there quite negatively.

It was pouring outside, and she simply wanted to take a long nap. The right side of the roof was leaking, as well as the left, and to her dismay, there was absolutely nothing to do. Sure, Grandpa had books lining the shelves, but the only one that seemed slightly familiar was , and she certainly didn't want to read about some Ishmael character and an enormous whale.

"Sarah?" Grandpa had finally woken up from his daily nap and seemed quite alert. "Go put your bathing suit on and grab the tackle box in the garage."

"The tackle box? Why the tackle box?" Sarah asked with a look of absurdity on her face.

She used to fish with Grandpa Morrie off the dock when she was a little girl, but the thought of casting a line now seemed awkward, considering the current status of their distant relationship.

"Yes, the tackle box," Grandpa said. "We're going fishing and you're going swimming."

Sarah looked distastefully at the ground. "We haven't fished in years, Grandpa. And I..." she stuttered, trying to think of a hurried excuse. "And I...can't swim."

"Can't swim, just because it is raining you 'can't swim.' Grandpa said with a stink eye. He knew she was lying. "Of course, you can swim. You're better in the water than you are on land."

That much was true. Sarah was an exceptional swimmer. "Fine," she said. "I'll swim and fish, but you have to bait my hook."

Sarah despised putting the wriggling worm on the hateful hook.

"Hop to it," Grandpa said. "The tackle box is on the left cabinet when you walk in through the back door to the garage."

Sarah walked toward the cool garage and was greeted by the smell of cedar and pine. The garage was old and made entirely out of wood. Sarah reached toward the cabinet and picked up the tackle box. Curiosity gnawed at her and she couldn't help looking inside. Flinging open the lid, Sarah noticed a thick envelope next to the rusty hooks that Grandpa had discarded. She slid the seal open with her nail and immediately began reading the first letter in sight.

>>>>

Sarah's eyes filled with excitement. Wealth! Wealth?! She couldn't help imagining all the possibilities, one of which was buying her very own water park. It would only take a little convincing, she thought to herself, giggling. Scrambling through the tackle box, she noticed many more letters...11 to be exact. All from the same person from the same engineering firm, Dan Mortimer. Why hadn't Grandpa responded? Or, had he? Sarah grabbed the box firmly, and bounded out the garage door. What should she say? She knew for a fact that this was something she wanted, but she was not so sure about her grandfather. Sarah rushed out on to the boat, trying to avoid eye contact with Grandpa Morrie. He took the two oars and started rowing out on to the shimmering lake. The rain had finally subsided, and a smile grew across his wrinkled face. When finally arriving at the fishing grounds, Sarah opened the tackle box and handed the letter to grandpa Morrie. Oddly this wild turn of events didn't seem to surprise Grandpa Morrie at all. He simply smiled at her and let out a faint laugh.

"Chip off the old block are you? Your father was always snooping around in other people's business."

Sarah looked at him with a furious fire burning in her eyes.

"Grandpa Morrie, if you uphold your end of the firm's offer, you could be rich."

Grandpa Morrie sighed, "Sarah, do you know what fracking can do to the environment?"

"No," she admitted quietly.

"I'll show you," Grandpa Morrie said. He opened his ice box and pulled out a rainbow trout that he had recently caught. "Do you see this beautiful fish? If I were to agree to the offer, there is a possibility that chemicals and oil could flood McGregor Lake and kill the fish and many more to come—along with this glorious environment that we live in."

He gazed out into the distance, with a sense of awe. Sarah gave a smile, signifying that she finally understood. She knew that in the future the environment might only get worse, along with people's thoughts of greed. She wanted to be the one who protected what was around them. She then jumped in the lake, enjoying the environment that she lived in—including the people around her and the wisdom they shared.

Grandpa Morrie peered over the boat and smiled. "I told you that you're better in the water than on land."

Sarah continued treading water and gazed at the sun. "Yes, Grandpa. I think I needed to be reminded of that—and more importantly, of you."

Grandfather and granddaughter smiled at the horizon, both realizing they had learned something that day—about each other and the beauty of the world surrounding them.

Nora Riley
Sixth Grade, Queen of All Saints

THE COURAGE OF OPHELIA
By Margaret Worden

Hogwarts School of Wizardry and Writing
Instructor: Shannon McCann

Chapter one: Cedric Diggory

By the morning, it was known all across the wizarding world. A boy named Cedric Diggory was dead, and Voldemort was back. At least, that was what the-boy-who-lived proclaimed, although the Ministry did its best to drown out his voice. According to the Ministry of Magic, Harry Potter was nothing more than a lying attention-seeker who was working with Albus Dumbledore to wreak havoc in the wizarding world. Maybe it was easier than accepting the truth. Not everyone believed the Ministry, however. Those who had been face-to-face with the destruction and death wrought by the first reign of Voldemort, those who had had their lives ripped apart, those who knew Voldemort's work when they saw it—they knew that Harry Potter lied about nothing.

Ophelia Williams was one of those people. She remembered the night when three Death Eaters broke into her house and murdered her family. How could she forget? The sounds of glass breaking, her mother telling her and her brother to hide, and her father, brave as he was, grabbing his wand to protect them before a green light stopped him in his tracks. She remembered watching through the keyhole in the closet door, praying that she wouldn't be found, nearly choking from the effort it took not to cry out when that same green light claimed her mother. She didn't cry though. Instead, she felt relieved when they didn't check the closet where she was hiding. They did check underneath the bed though. Where her little brother hid.

She remembered timidly coming out from that wretched closet, once the Death Eaters had left, sure that they had done what they came to do, and running, barefoot, out the front door, away from the broken mirrors and shadows of a once-happy family. The Order of the Phoenix had found her later and taken her in. Rhey had enrolled her at Hogwarts, and during the summer she had stayed with a member of the Order or had lived at headquarters. When she turned seventeen, they gave her the option of becoming a member of the Order herself, which she accepted in a heartbeat. She was ready. She would finally get her revenge. However, before she could even go on a mission, Voldemort was defeated, and the name Harry Potter became famous everywhere. Strangely, Ophelia was okay with not having to seek revenge any longer. She liked this new peace. Safety was a feeling that she could get used to. The Order disbanded, and everyone went their separate ways.

She moved to London, and opened a coffee shop in Diagon Alley. She grew comfortable, and although the guilt of surviving her family's deaths never left her, she was able to pretend that everything was fine. Until Cedric Diggory died, and Voldemort returned. She knew it was true, no matter how much she wished she could deny it. And with that knowledge, her world shattered once more.

Chapter Two: Not So Cowardly After All

You might think that she rushed back to the Order when everyone was called back. She wished she had. Instead, she ran away. Again. Like a Time and time again, she asked herself what the point was of joining the Order if she was just going to back down the moment there was any actual danger? She went into hiding, abandoning the Order and fleeing to a small seaside village. She had some money saved, Muggle money to be exact, and she used it to rent a small house on the beach. Not that it was the kind of beach that anyone would ever use on vacation. The sky was a menacing gray, the water was choppy enough to drown you, and it was windy enough to fly you away if you weren't heavy. Then again, it was late spring. Perhaps the beach was lovelier in the summertime. She hoped so.

It had been a few months since Ophelia had arrived in the small town, although she already knew many of the people that resided there. As she walked out of her house, bundled up in a heavy wool coat to protect against the cold winds that seemed to plague the town, she waved to the fishermen who were getting ready to head out on their boats. She admired their ability to go out on such dangerous waters. It certainly wasn't for the faint of heart. A small voice in her head chimed in: She silenced the voice. It would only bring her sorrow. As she walked into the supermarket, she pulled out a list. "All right, let's see... it looks like I need milk, bread, and sandwich fixings, like lettuce or bread, maybe some tomato."

An hour later, shopping done, Ophelia walked out of the supermarket and started to walk home. Before she could take so much as three steps however, a loud noise interrupted her thoughts. Her feet moved before she knew what was happening.

The little voice spoke in her head once more.

Ophelia silenced the voice, because if the sound had come from that house, she decided she wouldn't dwell on it. The house in question was that of the Abercrombie family, who were her friends and probably the only wizarding family in the village. Mrs. Abercrombie was a Muggle though, so a visit from some of Voldemort's followers wasn't out of the question, but Ophelia hoped she was wrong.

This family had been kind to her in the past few months, inviting her to dinners and picnics; she had even babysat their kids! She taught their son, Euan, who reminded her so painfully of her brother, to ride a broom. They couldn't suffer the same fate as her family! As she rounded the corner, the house came into view, and her worst fears were confirmed. There, floating in the sky over the house, was the Dark Mark mark. Once more her feet moved on their own. She ran into the house, wand raised and ready.

She wasn't prepared for the sight that greeted her. There, lying on the floor, were Mr. and Mrs. Abercrombie and their daughter, Lucy. All of them dead. She could feel the tears fall down her face before she realized she was crying. Wait. Euan wasn't there. She looked to her left. There, detained by one of the three Death Eaters that had started this murder, was Euan. If she had come any later, he would most likely would have already suffered the same fate as his family. Noticing her standing in the doorway, one of the Death Eaters raised his wand. She knew what he would say, so she said it first. " she yelled out.

This time the flash of green light came from her own wand. She didn't take the time to process what she had just done, although later she would be horrified by her actions. Instead she grabbed Euan and ran.

To be continued

Margaret Worden
Traverse City West High School, 9th Grade

DEAD BONES
By Eleanor Olds

Writing Stories That Rock
Instructor: Claire Alexander

The girl had long, blonde hair and soulful eyes. Her straight, white dress was ratty and skimmed the dead grass of the abandoned graveyard. A squirrel ran behind her on a quest for food, its paws crunching leaves as if they were bones. It wasn't common for animals to be around here. It was dry, and all the plants were dead. The graveyard had been abandoned a long while ago, just like the town nearby that had once been home to many happy people. Before the disease struck, that is. The town's inhabitants dropped like flies; the graveyard grew larger and larger until the remaining citizens came to their senses and bailed for the growing cities in the East. The smell of rotten leaves wafted through the air. The girl continued on her course. Her dirty bare feet hit sharp rocks, but she didn't flinch. It should have cut her feet open, but no blood surfaced, and the girl showed no pain. She closed her eyes and a small smile crept onto her lips as she began to hum. The song echoed through the dead forest. The girl began to skip, her eyes still closed.

Finally, the girl stopped and opened her mysterious eyes. She extended her long, ghostly pale fingers and lightly stroked the top of the gravestone in front of her. Her smile widened as she sensed the new presence behind her. She rose and turned to face the new girl behind her. She had black hair and light ivory skin, just like the blond girl.

"Hello, Claire, have you come to play another game?" The new girl asked. Claire smiled and put her pale palm against the other.

"Yes, Anne. So, we will be together forever and ever."

Claire entwined her fingers with Anne as they ran off to the old town, their giggles echoing through the dead forest.

A few leaves blew up against the gravestone Claire had touched. It read, "Anne Marie Smith, born 1790, died 1801 of disease."

A little while later, the squirrel that had passed Claire came to a gravestone. It had an odd smell to it; someone had recently been there. The gravestone read, "Claire Rose Smith, born 1791, died 1802 of disease. May you rest in peace with your cousin."

Eleanor Olds
East Middle School, 7th Grade

PERSPECTIVE
By Talon O'Brien

Writing Stories That Rock
Instructor: Claire Alexander

Perspective.
Perspective is a particular attitude toward or way of regarding something. An example: you think your neighbor is rude. That's a perspective. Got it?

So when I see a girl walk into class, my mind says She walks to the back of the room and sits down. As she does this, I feel someone tap my shoulder.

"Who is that?" a voice says. I turn around to see my friend Brady. "Her?" I motion my head toward the girl.

"No, the teacher," she said, rolling her eyes. "Yeah, the girl!"

"I don't know," I reply, "All I can tell is that she's...different." I take a look at the girl again. Tall, brown hair, blue eyes. I start to turn away, but I see something change with her. I look back to see what changed. Everything is the same except...

Her eyes. They weren't blue, they were green. And then they were brown, and then red...

"Hello?" Brady says, punching my shoulder.

"Huh?" I say, rubbing my shoulder. "What?"

"What about her is different?" she asks.

"Well, her eyes are ..."

"Okay class! Let's begin!" The teacher announces. He grabs a marker, and starts writing on the board. I turn back to her.

"Later."

I watch the teacher as I wonder about the girl and what she's doing here.

>>>>

The bell rings, and everyone rises from their seat. I turn toward Brady's direction and walk to her. I punch her shoulder to get her attention.

"Ow!" she exclaims, "What was that for?"

I shrug. "Payback."

She gives me a look of slight irritation. I roll my eyes, and continue.

"So, about the girl," I say, "Have you seen her eyes?"

"Yeah. They're green, right?" she asks, a hint of confusion.

"Yeah, for a few seconds they are. But then they're blue, and then brown, and then red. You see what I'm saying?" I say.

"Ha, ha, funny," she laughs, "That's not possible."

"Seriously! I'm not joking," I reply, "Go talk to her or something. You'll see. I'll see you at lunch, all right?"

"Yeah, fine," she waves, "See ya!"

I wave as I go to my locker. As I start unlocking the locker, I notice the kid next to me. He's completely motionless, staring at the locker in front of him. He just stands there, doing nothing.

"Hello?" I tap his shoulder, and he turns to me. I feel a chill run down my spine when I see his eyes. They were like the girl's.

Without saying anything, I grab my stuff and run to class.

>>>>

The bell finally rings, and I'm out of my seat. I rush to my locker, grab my stuff, and start to head to the cafeteria.

As I'm walking, I see Brady. I run up to her and start talking.

"Did you talk with her? Did you see her eyes?" I said, waiting for a response. I didn't get one.

"Brady?"

I see her looking at me with a blank stare.

"Oh no, not you!" I cry. Her eyes were changing colors, just like the other girl's. I back away slowly until I bump into someone. I look behind me, and I see the kid that was by his locker. I look all around, and I see people surrounding me, all with the changing eyes. I feel my face go pale.

All of a sudden, I see everyone come closer. And closer. And closer...

Something hits the back of my head, and I fall to the ground onto my back. The last thing I remember is the girl, standing over me, until I lose consciousness.

To be continued

Talon O'Brien
East Middle School, 8th Grade

FLOWERS FOR THE DEAD
By Hannah Abner

Writing Stories That Rock
Instructor: Claire Alexander

My hands were shoved in my pockets. I ignored their shaking. It was too soon to be coming here, yet here I was. Standing in the middle of rows upon rows of flowers, each representing a death of someone I knew, someone who died for my cause. I forced myself to walk but any control I had was lost when I reached the patch of daisies. I couldn't move. These small, delicate flowers symbolized little Mae. Mae, who didn't know what was going on, but was ready to wholeheartedly join us. Us, the rebellion against a society that destroyed little minds like hers. Mae who shouldn't have had to die. Mae who in every way, resembled a daisy. Innocent. Young. Simple.

Mae. 8 years old.

>>>>

I heard shouts and sharp noises that I recognized as gunshots. We heard them daily here. But this was different. For days, there had been whispers of an escape plan, and tonight was apparently the night it was going to happen. My roommate stood up. I didn't know her name or her age, and she didn't know mine. We weren't allowed to know that here at school. Well, I guess it was home as well because we never left. But she was the only one I had here, and she was the only one I needed. She was always nice to me, and I loved her like she was my own family.

"C'mon," she said, taking my hand. "We don't want to be left behind."

We left our room and were instantly swept along in the flow of bodies headed in the direction where we all knew the huge front doors to be. We couldn't move in any direction except forward. We thundered into the stairwell. Kids screamed and yelled. I heard popping noises. Gunshots. I felt people fall down behind me. I could smell the sweat and blood of hundreds of kids all packed into the small stairwell. All trying to escape. I couldn't breathe. I was so scared.

Somehow, in the chaos, I lost my grip on her hand. She slid behind me somewhere. I looked over my shoulder, trying to see where she went. She wasn't moving. Blood was oozing from her stomach; she had been shot. No. Wait. Why was everyone still running? Couldn't they see she needed help? She was shot! I had to get to her.

I tried to stop but I couldn't. I fought hard, but I was too tired from running. Bodies pushed me on from all sides. I screamed out but no one heard me. I jerked my head around trying to get another glimpse of her. I did. All I could see in the half of a second that I got was her eyes full of pain, and dark red blood staining her grey school uniform. She looked scared. I was, too. Tears stung my eyes. As I was pushed along, I cried for this girl whose name I had never known. She had given me comfort. She treated me like a sister. And now she was lost. She would never smile again, never hold my hand again. She was gone.

We reached the last stretch. Ahead of me, I could see the metal doors that had been forced open. I was almost there. Tears almost blinded me, but nothing could take away the sight of sun streaming in through the huge opening in the dark walls of this horrible place. There was more popping. More people fell. I was so close to the door, I could feel the outside. I could also feel my legs starting to give up. I was so tired. But I could smell the air. I could taste it. That was the only thing keeping me going. We were so close. And "pop." I went down.

I couldn't breathe. I couldn't feel anything. I was numb. I saw blood spreading across my chest and stomach at an alarming rate. My vision started to go blurry. This was it wasn't it? I wasn't going to make it out. I was going to join the hundreds of kids that failed to escape. I was going to see her again though. I saw a figure come into my sight. God, maybe.

"What's your name?" he asked in a quiet voice that I was somehow able to hear over the terrible noises around me.

"Mae," I managed.

"I'm Max. Don't worry, you're going to a better place. I won't forget you, Mae," the person whispered, and he stayed there, right in the middle of my field of vision, until the world went black.

To Be Continued

Hannah Abner
East Middle School, 8th Grade

FICTION
Saroiny Jordan Hosler

Camp Half-Blood
Instructor: Claire Alexander
Writing prompt: Imagine your favorite place in the world. It can be as personal as your house/bedroom or as big and grand as Disney World.

It may seem like a normal teenager's bedroom at first glance, but there is so much more than that. When you enter, the lights are always turned off, only a little bit of natural light coming in from the window, along with the dim light of a tiny lamp on the dresser next to the bed.

Some books are scattered all around the room, most in piles. In the midst of all the books, there is a girl. The habitat of the normal bedroom. She may seem a bit shy, reserved and secretive, but once you get to know her, she is only secretive. The reason is that there is one secret she must protect with her life. She glances around, making sure there is no one approaching. Then, she uses her magic to create a functional dummy of herself, sitting exactly where she was reading fan fiction. The girl smirked as she hissed out "Open," and a secret door revealing a passageway embedded in the wall silently opened. She entered and hissed "Close," and it closed behind her as she crept into the headquarters of the Triples Muertes, "The Triple Death." Her two comrades were approaching her. They nodded as they all put their robes on together and set out out to find their next target. Never doubt that what seems normal not normal, just like the normal bedroom the girl lives in. Now that you know there is a secret passage, it isn't that normal anymore, is it?

Saroiny Jordan Hosler
Traverse City Central High School, 9th Grade

FICTION
Makenzie Womack

Camp Half-Blood
Instructor: Claire Alexander
Writing prompt: Imagine your favorite place in the world. It can be as personal as your house/bedroom or as big and grand as Disney World.

Looking back at me is my reflection in a clouded window. Blurry outlines of leaves blow through the mist settling under a large pine tree. I attempt to open the glass door only to be greeted by a lock preventing my journey just like a brick wall. The sky grows a shade darker as the clouds become thicker with heavy rain drops desperately fighting against the gravitational pull of the Earth's core.

Giving up on the thought of leaving, I walk over to the cupboard that I used to find pleasure in organizing, though now that feels like a distant memory. Taped to the inside of the door are drawings and poems that were collected over the years. Closing the cabinet, tears prick behind my eyes.

I go back to the door, knowing full well nothing will happen, yet I attempt to open it once more. It still doesn't budge. In the corner of the open room there are three large stacks of stools. I decide to sit. The floor still seems to have its never-ending supply of dirt and dust that clings like wet jeans after falling into a creek.

Feeling a slight draft in the silent space as the breeze starts singing. The droplets of rain have finally grown tired of resisting the inevitable force of gravity; they splash against the window, sounding louder than a stampede in the hauntingly, quiet room.

Abandoned once again. The baby bird being pushed out of the comfortable safety of its nest and being forced to fly. Sitting on top of the towering stack of stools, which at one point was as dangerous as touching a burning flame. Now it seems dull. Without the fear of punishment looming overhead, anything is possible.

Pondering what to do next with this new freedom, which now doesn't seem like such a bad thing. The wind picks up again. Blowing the trees mercilessly from one corner of the sky to another. Attacking the exterior, causing the building to shift and sway with every gust.

"I'll make bottle rockets!" I exclaim with a devil's grin.

Walking over to the locked cabinet, I wonder how I am going to possibly open it, but it was obvious. The key was misplaced, but the door could still be opened wide enough without unlocking it.

After a good 10 minutes the supplies were gathered. The wind was still blowing and the door was still locked. I gathered 10 ml of vinegar, 8 ml baking soda, and 2 ml glitter into a film canister with as much efficiency as possible. The contained ingredients exploded, sending glitter all through the room.

Though this was quite satisfying for the moment, the room and its contents were covered with gloopy glitter and smelled overpoweringly of vinegar. "Probably not the best of ideas, but still totally worth it," I said to no one in particular, heading to the bathroom to clean up.

Presuming the power was still not working—there was no water or light—at least I could attempt to dry the vinegar splotches off of my gray hoodie with some paper towels. "All of this for the sake of vanity, and no one's here," I thought.

Pacing the halls and scanning the sky through the countless windows soon became too unbearable, as nothing changed anyway. So I decided to lie in the hall, ignoring the thin layer of dust.

Makenzie Womack
Traverse City West High School, 9th Grade

A EULOGY FOR THE COMMON SANDWICH
By Eli Pszczolkowski

Camp Half-Blood
Instructor: Claire Alexander
Writing prompt: Write a eulogy for a sandwich, from being ordered to being eaten.

Birth into a cruel world. Put together by the plastic gloves of a giant, nay, a deity. His heart was made of beef and lettuce and he was all the better for it. In his short life, he had brought love and joy to so many, but his life was tragically ended by the teeth of the very one who created him. You will be dearly missed, Cornelius Romaine II.

Eli Pszczolkowski
Traverse City East Middle School, 8th Grade

R.I.P. BLT ~ MARCH 14, 2018 - MARCH 14, 2018
By Nathaniel Myers

Camp Half-Blood
Claire Alexander
Writing prompt: Write a eulogy for a sandwich, from being ordered to being eaten.

We are here tonight to honor the life of Barthalomew Leslie Toomes, known by his nickname "BLT." Born in a New York deli on March 14, 2018, Bart had dreams from a young age of becoming a dentist. He always made Jeff and Bertha, his parents and employers, so proud, with his friendliness and willingness to get along with other bread types when racial tensions were high. Then came the Great Sandwich Massacre of March 14, 2018, when a man ordered 4 footlongs, 3 meatball subs, 5 turkey Italianos, and 6 BLTs. Bart's parents gave him to a murderer for $2.99, and Bart, wanting to check out the man's teeth, jumped into his mouth. As the fatal accident occurred, he was crushed into crumbs. BLT was a friendly and loyal boy who was delicious, nutritious and will be remembered well. May he rest in peace.

**Nathaniel Myers,
West High School, 9th Grade**

SNAPE'S CHILDHOOD
By Kristen May

Hogwarts School of Wizardry and Writing
Instructor: Shannon McCann

Snape pulls his black robe over his head and trudges downstairs. This is his third year at Hogwarts and he is not looking forward to it. To be fair, he never really looks forward to Hogwarts. Snape has a reputation for being grumpy and today is no different. His mother is already downstairs setting out a plate of burned toast and burnt eggs. Snape shoves it down and washes it down with some gruel. His mother starts humming a tune and Snape stares at her, incredulous. Usually the only reason she talks to him is to give him something to do. His mother places her hands on his shoulders and practically shoves him out the door. "Don't want to be late," she calls and slams the door in his face. Snape sighs and starts walking toward the train station.

Snape walks through the wall that separates the Muggle train from the Wizard train. He sees all the parents hugging their children and scowls.

"Love is a weakness," his mother has always told him. "Don't fall into its trap."

[We join Snape later in the story at Hogwarts.]

In the hallway Snape passed by his friend Lily, and she put a note in his hand. It said:

Meet me outside in five minutes. Got to talk.

Sincerely, Lily

He grinned and went to meet her outside. She was already there, working on some homework underneath a big tree. She looked up and smiled when she saw him. Snape made his way over to her and sat down beside her. There was a bit of silence before either of them said anything. Snape looked up and asked her, "What did you want to talk about?"

Lily looked at him and said, "I just wanted to see if anything was going on."

He was about to respond when it suddenly got cold. The sky turned black and Snape knew what was coming. He was about to grab for Lily's hand, but he felt nothing. He slowly turned his head and saw nothing. Lily was gone.

Snape rushed into Hogwarts and ran to Dumbledore's office. He arrived, breathless, to see all the teachers huddled around each other, talking. Professor Winter McFuzz saw him first and smiled, showing all his teeth. "Ah, Severus Snape, yes?" Snape nodded, too out of breath to form any words.

"Are you all right?" Professor McGonagall asked him in concern.

"Lily... gone... kidnapped."

Dumbledore immediately stood up and came over to him. He put a comforting arm around Snape's shoulders and guided him to the door.

"You must be awfully tired," he said in a low voice. "Why don't you get some rest?"

He pushed Snape out of his office and shut the door in his face. Snape stared at the closed door, wondering what the teachers were discussing before he started shuffling toward his room. A nap did sound good.

When morning arrived, Snape sleepily sat up and yawned. His mind was blank until all of it came rushing back to him and he suddenly felt exhausted again. He considered going back to bed until his stomach growled and he realized that he had skipped dinner. He washed himself up and changed into his clothes. After getting his bags he started down toward the Great Hall. When he entered everyone stopped eating and looked at him.

"I heard that he was the kid who was with Lily when she disappeared," said a kid with glasses.

Snape bowed his head in embarrassment and walked quickly through the Great Hall. He took a seat, aware of the kids still staring at him, and started eating. He missed Lily terribly and he wished she were here now, sitting by his side.

In his potions class, he finally made a decision. He was going after Lily. He doesn't know what made him decide that, but he was suddenly overcome with a feeling of courage. After class he was thinking to himself when a kid with glasses walked up to him. He offered his hand and said, "James Potter."

Snape just stared at him confused. James cleared his throat and said, "I liked Lily too, and I want to save her so if you have a plan, I'm in."

Snape just stared at him, not comprehending what James was saying. "What?" Snape stammered.

"I liked Lily and I want to save her so if you have a plan, I'm in," James repeated, starting to get irritated.

"Um," Snape said, still not understanding what James is saying.

"Are you actually going to talk or are you just going to say 'what' and 'um' like a blubbering idiot," James snapped, temper frayed.

"Meet me outside at lunch?" Snape asked.

"Perfect," James said, composure restored, and walked away.

Snape stared after him, still not knowing what just happened.

At lunch Snape walked out to find James already sitting beneath a tree. He walked over to him and plopped down. James looked up and asked him, "What's your plan?"

Snape flushed and mumbled, "Find where Voldemort is keeping her and rescue her."

James looked at him and said, "Why Voldemort?"

Snape showed him Voldemort's picture in a book. James gasped and said, "He looks evil."

Snape had to force down a laugh because you'd have to be blind to not see that.

"Yeah," he said. "He does look evil."

"Well, when do you want to do this?" James asked him.

"I was thinking tonight," Snape said and looked down at his shoes.

"Perfect," James replied and walked into the school. Snape stared after him, wondering what he had just done.

>>>>

When Snape entered Hogwarts, he ran into Professor Winter McFuzz on his way down the hall.

"Oh, sorry," Snape said, and bent down to pick up his books. Then his head collided with Professor Winter McFuzz's head, because his professor had also leaned down to pick up Snape's books.

"Sorry," Snape said again, and he held his breath, waiting for a scolding.

Instead Professor Winter McFuzz just laughed and took Snape by his shoulders.

"My dear boy, it is all right. What I was meaning to ask is if you would be interested in helping me teach transfiguration class. You are so good at the spells, and it would be a real help if you could."

Snape looked at him and then said to the floor, "I'm kind of busy, but maybe a different time?"

"Oh," Professor Winter McFuzz. A brief shadow crossed over his face, but then it was gone. "That's all right, my boy. Another time then."

He slapped Snape on the back and walked off.

When the rest of his house had gone to bed, Snape slipped out of his bed and tiptoed outside. He was supposed to meet James by the tree where they'd met earlier that day, but he didn't see him anywhere. He sat down and leaned against the tree. He was just considering going back to sleep when James came walking down the hill. Snape got up and they walked toward the lake. They had decided earlier to take a boat and then use magic once they were out of Hogwarts. James got in the front and Snape got in the back. James started to use his magic, but Snape punched him in the back and whispered, "Stop! We can't use magic!" James gave him a dirty look, but Snape ignored it and started to row. James eventually started to row, too, and the little boat made its way across the lake.

Snape stepped out of the boat and onto a marsh. James was in front of him and silently the two boys begin picking their way across the marsh. Sometime later, they finally stepped on dry land. Snape was picking mud off his shoes when he felt James tap him on his shoulder. He looked up and saw an old abandoned shack.

Snape gulped and considered going back. They shouldn't have to do this. The teachers should be here, not them. But then he thought of Lily and he started walking toward the shack. The full moon shone down on them and somewhere an owl hooted. Snape paused at the door and looked back to see James behind him.

"Open the door," James whispered, and Snape did exactly that.

They stepped into the room and the first thing that hit Snape was the smell. It smelled like old socks and rotten eggs. Not a good combination. Snape walked farther in and whispered to James, "This is spooky."

No one replied. He looked behind him and saw an empty space.

James was gone. Snape looked around, thinking that someone was going to jump out at him. But no one did. At least now he knew that someone was here. Snape ventured farther into the room holding his wand out. It was the third room that he found what he was looking for. There was Lily, tied to a chair and gagged.

"Lily" Snape said. "Thank goodness you're safe." Lily was pushing against the rope, shouting something into her gag.

"What?" Snape said, starting to turn around. But it was too late! A spell hit him and then he saw ... nothing.

To be continued

Kristen May
Woodland School, 7th Grade

FIFTH GRADE POETRY WORKSHOPS

GOODNIGHT WORLD
Aveelee Frantz

Poetry Workshop Instructor: Sam Collier
Classroom Instructor: Shannon Cobb

I lay down eyes wide
open.

Eyes tired unable to
close.

Calming music and exciting
voices play all night.

Now I look out my window.

The sky is starting to glow
Seems I've stayed up.

I guess it's time to say sorry and
Goodnight, I'm truly tired.

Aveelee Frantz
Traverse Heights Elementary, 5th Grade

MY DOG
Thomas Monroe

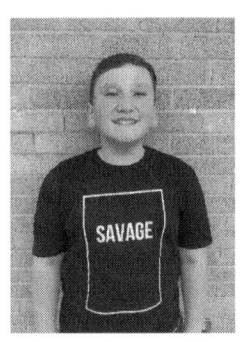

Poetry Workshop Instructor: Sam Collier
Classroom Instructor: Caitlin Thomas

My Dog is strong and good
He would follow me I would follow him
We went for walks
At the beach
We played fetch at my house
When I went to my grandma's
House my dog is happy to see me
And my grandma's house smells like
Candles and hard candy
And my grandma's house looks
Old but it's my house too
And I love it I play with my
Dog I leave 3 months we get
A call everything drops in my life
My dog died
But he's in a good
Place now
I miss him he misses me
I love him.

Thomas Monroe
Traverse Heights Elementary, 5th Grade

THE WET BLIZZARD
Nataliya Gorokhovskiy

Poetry Workshop Instructor: Sam Collier
Classroom Instructor: Laurie Lijewsky

When it begins to snow then it is
like a wet and white blizzard it is
so chilly the minute you go outside
then your cheeks turn as red as a
tomato. You start to shiver but when
you come inside to the warm fireplace
and touch the warm cup of hot
chocolate, it is so warm and cozy that
you are about to fall asleep because
you are no longer shivering.

Nataliya Gorokhovskiy
Blair Elementary, 5th Grade

Made in the USA
Middletown, DE
22 May 2019